SHAMBHALA CLASSICS

Bhagavan Śrī Ramana Maharshi

The Spiritual Teaching of RAMANA MAHARSHI

FOREWORD BY C. G. JUNG

SHAMBHALA
Boston & London
2004

Shambhala Publications, Inc.
Horticultural Hall
300 Massachusetts Avenue
Boston, Massachusetts 02115
www.shambhala.com

13 12 11 10 9 8 7 6 5

Printed in the United States of America

⊗This edition is printed on acid-free paper that meets the American National Standards Institute Z39.48 Standard.
♻This book was printed on 30% postconsumer recycled paper. For more information please visit www.shambhala.com.
Distributed in the United States by Random House, Inc., and in Canada by Random House of Canada Ltd

The Library of Congress Catalogues the previous edition of this book as follows:

Ramana, Maharshi.
The spiritual teaching of Ramana Maharshi.
1.Spiritual life (Hinduism) I. Title.
[BL1237.36.R35 1988] 294.5'448 88-18220
ISBN 978-0-87773-024-8 (pbk.)
ISBN 978-1-59030-139-5 (Shambhala Classics)

Contents

PREFACE vii

FOREWORD BY C. G. JUNG ix

BIOGRAPHICAL SKETCH xiii

WHO AM I? 1

SPIRITUAL INSTRUCTION 13

- Instruction 15
- Practice 19
- Experience 31
- Attainment 34

MAHARSHI'S GOSPEL 39

- Work and Renunciation 41
- Silence and Solitude 48
- Mind Control 50
- Bhakti and Jñāna 55
- Self and Individuality 57
- Self-Realization 61
- Guru and His Grace 65
- Peace and Happiness 71
- Self-Inquiry 73
- Sādhana and Grace 80
- The Jñāni and the World 84
- The Heart Is the Self 91
- Aham and Aham-vṛtti 101

NOTES 109

GLOSSARY 111

Preface

A gently indrawn breath—with no thought—can bring the ecstasy of total awareness—beyond words.

In these three books of answers to inquirers, Bhagavan Ramana Maharshi, without offending common sense, reason or logic, has come as close as possible to saying the unsayable and points the way—innumerable ways—for You to find the Self and Be.

To Understand the Ultimate—experience must be Intimate.

Beyond that which you think is that which you are. Realizing this does not involve specific practices or attitudes other than Understanding. No withdrawal is necessary—no change of present time, place or condition—only a change of viewpoint, which you bring about yourself for your Self.

A recent letter from S. S. Cohen says: "'Be' sums up the whole practical teaching of Bhagavan. There is nothing in the material life to compensate for it—neither wealth, sex, art, science nor any other ideal. It is the Greatest Good—the bliss and truth absolute."

Bhagavan found Enlightenment for himself without a physical guru.

In these books of questions, asked and answered, may you find your answer. This can be a trip to end all trips. Find out who you are and you can't help but Be! Know that you immortal Are and you have but to Be.

May all beings be well, may all beings be happy.

Peace, peace.
PEACE

Joe & Guinevere Miller

Foreword

Śrī Ramana and His Message to Modern Man

Śrī Ramana is a true son of the Indian earth. He is genuine and, in addition to that, something quite phenomenal. In India he is the whitest spot in a white space.

What we find in the life and teachings of Śrī Ramana is the purest of India; with its breath of world-liberated and liberating humanity, it is a chant of millenniums. This melody is built up on a single, great motif, which, in a thousand colorful reflexes, rejuvenates itself within the Indian spirit, and the latest incarnation of which is Śrī Ramana Maharshi himself.

The identification of the Self with God will strike the European as shocking. It is a specifically Oriental realization, as expressed in Śrī Ramana's utterances. Psychology cannot contribute anything further to it, except the remark that it lies far beyond its scope to propose such a thing. However, it is clear to the Indian that the Self as spiritual Source is not different from God; and in so far as man abides in his Self, he is not only contained in God but is God Himself. Śrī Ramana is quite clear in this respect.

The Goal of Eastern practices is the same as that of Western mysticism: the focus is shifted from the "I" to the Self, from man to God. This means that the "I" disappears in the Self, and the man in God. A similar effort is described in the *exercitia spiritualia,* in which the "personal property," the "I" subjugate to the highest possible degree to the possessorship of Christ. Śrī Ramakrishna adopted the same position in regard to the Self, only with him the dilemma between the "I" and the Self comes a little more closely to the foreground. Śrī Ramana declares unmistakably that the real purpose of spiritual practice is the dissolution of the "I." Ramakrishna, however, shows a somewhat hesitating attitude in this respect. Though he says, "As long as the I-sense lasts, so long are true Knowledge (*jñāna*) and Liberation (*mukti*) impossible," yet he must acknowledge the fatal nature of *ahaṃkāra*. He says, "How very few can obtain this Union (*samādhi*) and free themselves from this 'I'? It is very rarely possible. Talk as much as you want, isolate yourself continuously, still this 'I' will always return to you. Cut down the poplar tree today, and you will find tomorrow it forms new shoots. When you ultimately find that this 'I' cannot be destroyed, let it remain as 'I' the servant." In relation to this concession, Śrī Ramana is certainly the more radical.

The changing relations between these two quantities, the "I" and the Self, represent a field of experience which the introspective consciousness of the East has explored to a degree almost unattainable by the Western human being. The philosophy of the East, which is so very different from ours, represents to us a highly valuable present, which, however, we "must obtain in order to possess." Śrī Ramana's words once again sum up the principal things which the Spirit of India has accumulated during thousands of years in contemplation of the Inner Self; and the individual life and work of the Maharshi exemplifies once more the innermost striving of the Indian people to find the liberating original Source.

The Eastern nations are threatened by a quick disintegration of their spiritual goods, and what comes into their place cannot always be considered to belong to the best of the Western mind. Therefore, one may look upon sages like Śrī Ramakrishna and Śrī Ramana as modern prophets. They not only remind us of the thousands-of-years-old spiritual culture of India, but also directly embody it. Their life and teachings form an impressive warning not to forget the demand of the soul in all the new things of Western civilization and their materialistic-technical and commercial concerns of the world. The breathless impulse to obtain and possess in the political, social and intellectual fields, which is rummaging the apparent, unappeasable passion in the soul of the Westerner, is also spreading continuously in the East and threatens to bear consequences not yet to be overlooked. Not only in India but also in China, much has already been lost in which once the life of the soul lived and flourished. The externalization-culture of the West can truly clear away many evils, the destruction of which seems to be very desirable and advantageous. But, as experience has shown, this progress is bought too dearly with a loss of spiritual culture. It is undoubtedly more comfortable to dwell in a well-ordered and hygienically furnished house, but that does not answer the question as to *who* is the dweller in this house, and whether his soul enjoys a similar state of order and purity, that is, like that of the house serving for external life. Once man is set to the pursuit of external things, he is never satisfied, as experience shows, with the mere necessities of life, but always strives after more and more, which, true to his prejudices, he always seeks in external things. He forgets entirely that in spite of all external success inwardly he remains the same, and therefore complains of his poverty when he owns only one motor car instead of two like others around him. Certainly, the external life of man can bear many improvements and beautifications, but they lose their significance to the extent to which the inner man cannot keep up with them. The provision with all "necessities" is, without doubt, a source of happiness which is not to be underestimated. But above and beyond it, the inner man raises his claim, which cannot be satisfied by any external goods: and the less this voice is heard in the hunt for "the wonderful things" of this world, the more the inner man becomes a source of inexplicable bad luck and ununderstandable unhappiness in the midst of conditions of life from which one would expect something quite different. The externalization leads to an incurable suffering, because nobody can understand how one could suffer because of one's own nature. Nobody is surprised at his own insatiability, but looks upon it as his birthright; he does not realize that the one-sidedness of the diet of his soul ultimately leads to the most serious disturbances of balance. It is this which forms the illness of the Westerner, and he does not rest till he has infected the whole world with his greedy restlessness.

The wisdom and mysticism of the East have, therefore, a very great deal to tell us, provided they speak in their own inimitable speech. They should remind us of what we possess in our own culture of similar things and have already forgotten, and direct our attention to that which we put aside as unimportant, namely the destiny of our inner man. The life and teachings of Śrī Ramana are important not only for the Indian but also for the Westerner. Not only do they form a record of great human interest, but also a warning message to a humanity which threatens to lose itself in the chaos of its unconsciousness and lack of self-control.

C. G. Jung

The Foreword by C. G. Jung was originally published as the Foreword to Heinrich Zimmer's *Der Weg zum Selbst* and was translated by R. F. C. Hull in volume 11 of the *Collected Works* of C. G. Jung. Used by permission of Princeton University Press, publishers of the Bollingen Series.

A Biographical Sketch

Ramana Maharshi (1879–1950) was one of the greatest spiritual teachers of modern-day India. At the age of seventeen he attained a profound experience of the true Self without the guidance of a Guru and thereafter remained conscious of his identity with the Absolute (*Brahman*) at all times. After some years of silent seclusion he finally began to reply to the questions put to him by spiritual seekers all over the world. He followed no particular traditional system of teaching, but rather spoke directly from his own experience of nonduality. Ramana Maharshi wrote virtually nothing; his teaching took the form of conversations with visitors seeking his guidance (as transcribed by followers), the brief instructions he left with his followers, and a few songs. His method of instruction was to direct the questioner again and again to his true self and to recommend, as a path to realization, a tireless form of self-inquiry featuring the question "Who am I?" The transcribed conversations of Ramana Maharshi are known among spiritual seekers the world over and prized for their great inspirational power, which transcends all religious differences.

Śrī Ramana Maharshi was born on 29 December 1879 in Tiruchuli, Tamil Nadu (South India), the son of Shundaram Ayyar, a scribe and country lawyer; he was given the name Venkatarāman, abbreviated as Ramana. At the age of seventeen he suddenly had an experience of death one day in which he realized that the body dies but the consciousness is not touched by death. "I" am immortal consciousness. "All these," he later reported, "were no idle speculations. They went through me like a powerful, living truth that I experienced directly, almost without thinking. 'I' [i.e., the true I or Self] was reality, the only reality in this momentary state. All conscious activity that was related to my body flowed into this 'I.' From that moment, all attention was drawn as if by powerful magic to the 'I' or the 'Self.' The fear of death was permanently extinguished. From this time on I remained fully absorbed in the 'Self.'"

After this experience Venkatarāman lost all interest in things of the world and ultimately left home without his parents' permission, to find his way to the holy mountain of Arunāchala. There he spent several years in silent Self-absorption, first in a dark corner of a temple in Tiruvannāmalai, at the foot of the mountain, and later in various caves on the mountain itself; during this time he totally neglected all care of the body and at one point was virtually chewed up by insects. Even when his mother sought him out and attempted to get him to return home, he did not break his silence but rather acted as though he did not see her. When his followers begged him to make some response to his mother's desperate pleas, he wrote the following impersonal words on a scrap of paper: "The fate of the soul is determined in accordance with its *prārabdha-karma.* What is not meant to happen will not happen, however much you wish it. What is meant to happen will happen, no matter what you do to prevent it. This is certain. Therefore the best path is to remain silent."

When Ramana Maharshi later broke his silence and began to respond to questions about the path to the Self, an *āśrama* grew up around him in Tiruvannāmalai. There, in 1950, ill with cancer, Ramana Maharshi passed into *mahāsamādhi.* The site is still visited today by spiritual seekers of every nationality as a place of pilgrimage where the presence of the great saint can still be felt.

Adapted from the entry "Ramana Mahar(i)shi" by Kurt Friedrichs, in *The Encyclopedia of Eastern Philosophy and Religion* (Boston: Shambhala Publications, 1988).

WHO AM I?

Who Am I?

(Nān Yār?)

As all living beings desire to be happy always, without misery, as in the case of everyone there is observed supreme love for one's self, and as happiness alone is the cause for love, in order to gain that happiness which is one's nature and which is experienced in the state of deep sleep where there is no mind, one should know one's self. For that, the path of knowledge, the inquiry of the form "Who am I?," *is the principal means.*

1. *Who am I?*

The gross body, which is composed of the seven humors (*dhātus*), I am not; the five cognitive sense organs, i.e., the senses of hearing, touch, sight, taste, and smell, which apprehend their respective objects, i.e., sound, touch, color, taste, and odor, I am not; the five conative sense organs, i.e., the organs of speech, locomotion, grasping, excretion, and procreation, which have as their respective functions speaking, moving, grasping, excreting, and enjoying, I am not; the five vital airs, *prāṇa*, etc., which perform respectively the five functions of in-breathing, etc., I am not; even the mind which thinks, I am not; the nescience too, which is endowed only with the residual impressions of objects, and in which there are no objects and no functions, I am not.

2. *If I am none of these, then who am I?*

After negating all of the above-mentioned as "not this, not this," that Awareness which alone remains—that I am.

3. *What is the nature of Awareness?*

The nature of Awareness is existence-consciousness-bliss.

4. *When will the realization of the Self be gained?*

When the world which is what-is-seen has been removed, there will be realization of the Self, which is the seer.

5. *Will there not be realization of the Self even while the world is there (taken as real)?*

There will not be.

6. *Why?*

The seer and the object seen are like the rope and the snake. Just as the knowledge of the rope which is the substrate will not arise unless the false knowledge of the illusory serpent goes, so the realization of the Self which is the substrate will not be gained unless the belief that the world is real is removed.

7. *When will the world, which is the object seen, be removed?*

When the mind, which is the cause of all cognitions and of all actions, becomes quiescent, the world will disappear.

8. *What is the nature of the mind?*

What is called mind is a wondrous power residing in the Self. It causes all thoughts to arise. Apart from thoughts, there is no such thing as mind. Therefore, thought is the nature of mind. Apart from thoughts, there is no independent entity called the world. In deep sleep there are no thoughts, and there is no world. In the states of waking and dream, there are thoughts, and there is a world also. Just as the spider emits the thread (of the web) out of itself and again withdraws it into itself, likewise the mind projects the world out of itself and again resolves it into itself. When the mind comes out of the Self, the world appears. Therefore, when the world appears (to be real), the Self does not appear; and when the Self appears (shines), the world does not appear. When one persistently inquires into the nature of the mind, the mind will end leaving the Self (as the residue). What is referred to as the Self is the *Ātman*. The mind always exists only in dependence on something gross; it cannot stay alone. It is the mind that is called the subtle body or the soul (*jīva*).

9. *What is the path of inquiry for understanding the nature of the mind?*

That which rises as "I" in this body is the mind. If one inquires as to where in the body the thought "I" rises first, one would discover that it rises in the heart. That is the place of the mind's origin. Even if one thinks constantly "I," "I," one will be led to that place. Of all the thoughts that arise in the mind, the "I" thought is the first. It is only after the rise of this that the other thoughts arise. It is after the appearance of the first personal pronoun that the second and third personal pronouns appear; without the first personal pronoun there will not be the second and third.

10. *How will the mind become quiescent?*

By the inquiry "Who am I?" The thought "Who am I?" will destroy all other thoughts, and, like the stick used for stirring the burning pyre, it will itself in the end get destroyed. Then there will arise Self-realization.

11. *What is the means for constantly holding on to the thought "Who am I?"?*

When other thoughts arise, one should not pursue them, but should inquire: "To whom did they arise?" It does not matter how many thoughts arise. As each thought arises, one should inquire with diligence, "To whom has this thought arisen?" The answer that would emerge would be "To me." Thereupon, if one inquires "Who am I?," the mind will go back to its source, and the thought that arose will become quiescent. With repeated practice in this manner, the mind will develop the skill to stay in its source. When the mind that is subtle goes out through the brain and the sense organs, the gross names and forms appear; when it stays in the heart, the names and forms disappear. Not letting the mind go out but retaining it in the Heart is what is called "inwardness" (*antar-mukha*). Letting the mind go out of the Heart is known as "externalization" (*bahir-mukha*). Thus, when the mind stays in the Heart, the "I" which is the source of all thoughts will go and the Self which ever exists will shine. Whatever one does, one should do without the egoity "I." If one acts in that way, all will appear as of the nature of Shiva (God).

12. *Are there no other means for making the mind quiescent?*

Other than inquiry, there are no adequate means. If through other means it is sought to control the mind, the mind will appear to be controlled, but will again go forth. Through the control of breath also, the mind will become quiescent; but it will be quiescent only so long as the breath remains controlled, and when the breath resumes, the mind also will again start moving and will wander as impelled by residual impressions. The source is the same for both mind and breath. Thought, indeed, is the nature of the mind. The thought "I" is the first thought of the mind; and that is egoity. It is from that whence egoity originates that breath also originates. Therefore, when the mind becomes quiescent, the breath is controlled, and when the breath is controlled the mind becomes quiescent. But in deep sleep, although the mind becomes quiescent, the breath does not stop. This is because of the will of God, so that the body may be preserved and other people may not be under the impression that it is dead. In the state of waking and in *samādhi*, when the mind becomes quiescent the breath is controlled. Breath is the gross form of mind. Till the time of death, the mind keeps breath in the body; and when the body dies the mind takes the breath along with it. Therefore, the exercise of breath control is only an aid for rendering the mind quiescent (*manonigraha*); it will not destroy the mind (*manonāśa*).

Like the practice of breath control, meditation on the forms of God, repetition of mantras, restriction on food, etc., are but aids for rendering the mind quiescent.

Through meditation on the forms of God and through repetition of mantras, the mind becomes one-pointed. The mind will always be wandering. Just as when the chain is given to an elephant to hold in its trunk it will go along grasping the chain and nothing else, so also when the mind is occupied with a name or form it will grasp that alone. When the mind expands in the form of countless thoughts, each thought becomes weak; but as thoughts get resolved the mind becomes one-pointed and strong; for such a mind Self-inquiry will become easy. Of all the restrictive rules, that relating to the taking of sattvic food in moderate quantities is best; by observing this rule, the sattvic quality of mind will increase, and that will be helpful to Self-inquiry.

13. *The residual impressions (thoughts) of objects appear unending like the waves of an ocean. When will all of them be removed?*

As the meditation on the Self rises higher and higher, the thoughts will get destroyed.

14. *Is it possible for the residual impressions of objects that come from beginningless time, as it were, to be resolved, and for one to remain as the pure Self?*

Without yielding to the doubt "Is it possible or not?," one should persistently hold on to the meditation on the Self. Even if one be a great sinner, one should not worry and weep "Oh! I am a sinner, how can I be saved?"; one should completely renounce the thought "I am a sinner" and concentrate keenly on meditation on the Self; then one would surely succeed. There are not two minds—one good and the other evil; the mind is only one. It is the residual impressions that are of two kinds—auspicious and inauspicious. When the mind is under the influence of auspicious impressions it is called good; and when it is under the influence of inauspicious impressions it is regarded as evil.

The mind should not be allowed to wander toward worldly objects and what concerns other people. However bad other people may be, one should bear no hatred for them. Both desire and hatred should be eschewed. All that one gives to others one gives to one's self. If this truth is understood, who will not give to others? When one's self arises, all arises; when one's self becomes quiescent, all becomes quiescent. To the extent we behave with humility, to that extent there will result good. If the mind is rendered quiescent, one may live anywhere.

15. *How long should inquiry be practiced?*

As long as there are impressions of objects in the mind, so long the inquiry "Who am I?" is required. As thoughts arise they should be destroyed then and there in the very place of their origin, through inquiry. If one resorted to contemplation of the Self unintermittently, until the Self was gained, that alone would do. As long as there are enemies within the fortress, they will continue to sally forth; if they are destroyed as they emerge, the fortress will fall into our hands.

16. *What is the nature of the Self?*

What exists in truth is the Self alone. The world, the individual soul, and God are appearances in it, like silver in mother-of-pearl; these three appear at the same time and disappear at the same time.

The Self is that where there is absolutely no "I" thought. That is called Silence. The Self itself is the world; the Self itself is "I"; the Self itself is God; all is Shiva, the Self.

17. *Is not everything the work of God?*

Without desire, resolve, or effort, the sun rises; and in its mere presence, the sun-stone emits fire, the lotus blooms, water evaporates; people perform their various functions and then rest. Just as in the presence of the magnet the needle moves, it is by virtue of the mere presence of God that the souls governed by the three (cosmic) functions or the fivefold divine activity perform their actions and then rest, in accordance with their respective karmas. God has no resolve; no karma attaches itself to Him. This is like worldly actions not affecting the sun, or like the merits and demerits of the other four elements not affecting the all-pervading ether.

18. *Of the devotees, who is the greatest?*

He who gives himself up to the Self that is God is the most excellent devotee. Giving one's self up to God means remaining constantly in the Self without giving room for the rise of any thoughts other than the thought of the Self.

Whatever burdens are thrown on God, He bears them. Since the supreme power of God makes all things move, why should we, without submitting ourselves to it, constantly worry ourselves with thoughts as to what should be done and how, and what should not be done and how not? We know that the train carries all loads, so after getting on it why should we carry our small luggage on our head to our discomfort, instead of putting it down in the train and feeling at ease?

19. *What is nonattachment?*

As thoughts arise, destroying them utterly without any residue in the very place of their origin is nonattachment. Just as the pearl-diver ties a stone to his waist, sinks to the bottom of the sea and there takes the pearls, so each one of us should be endowed with nonattachment, dive within himself and obtain the Self-Pearl.

20. *Is it not possible for God and the Guru to effect the release of a soul?*

God and the Guru will only show the way to release; they will not by themselves take the soul to the state of release.

In truth, God and the Guru are not different. Just as the prey which has fallen into the jaws of a tiger has no escape, so those who have come within the ambit of the Guru's gracious look will be saved by the Guru and will not get lost; yet each one should by his own effort pursue the path shown by God or Guru and gain release. One can know oneself only with one's own eye of knowledge, and not with somebody else's. Does he who is Rama require the help of a mirror to know that he is Rama?

21. *Is it necessary for one who longs for release to inquire into the nature of the categories* (tattvas)?

Just as one who wants to throw away garbage has no need to analyze it and see what it is, so one who wants to know the Self has no need to count the number of categories or inquire into their characteristics; what he has to do is to reject altogether the categories that hide the Self. The world should be considered like a dream.

22. *Is there no difference between waking and dream?*

Waking is long and a dream short; other than this there is no difference. Just as waking happenings seem real while awake, so do those in a dream while dreaming. In dream the mind takes on another body. In both waking and dream states, thoughts, names, and forms occur simultaneously.

23. *Is it any use reading books for those who long for release?*

All the texts say that in order to gain release one should render the mind quiescent; therefore their conclusive teaching is that the mind should be rendered quiescent; once this has been understood there is no need for endless reading. In order to quiet the mind one has only to inquire within oneself what one's Self is; how could this search be done in books? One should know one's Self with one's own eye of wisdom. The Self is within the five sheaths; but books are outside them. Since the Self has to be inquired into by discarding the five sheaths, it is futile to search for it in books. There will come a time when one will have to forget all that one has learned.

24. *What is happiness?*

Happiness is the very nature of the Self; happiness and the Self are not different. There is no happiness in any object of the world. We imagine through our ignorance that we derive happiness from objects. When the mind goes out, it experiences misery. In truth, when its desires are fulfilled, it returns to its own place and enjoys the happiness that is the Self. Similarly, in the states of sleep, *samādhi*, and fainting, and when the object desired is obtained or the object disliked is removed, the mind becomes inward-turned and enjoys pure Self-happiness. Thus the mind moves without rest, alternately going out of the Self and returning to it. Under the tree the shade is pleasant; out in the open the heat is scorching. A person who has been going about in the sun feels cool when he reaches the shade. Someone who keeps on going from the shade into the sun and then back into the shade is a fool. A wise man stays permanently in the shade. Similarly, the mind of the one who knows the truth does not leave *Brahman*. The mind of the ignorant, on the contrary, revolves in the world, feeling miserable, and for a little time returns to *Brahman* to experience happiness. In fact, what is called the world is only thought. When the world disappears, i.e., when there is no thought, the mind experiences happiness; and when the world appears, it goes through misery.

25. *What is wisdom-insight* (jñāna-dṛṣṭi)?

Remaining quiet is what is called wisdom-insight. To remain quiet is to resolve the mind in the Self. Telepathy, knowing past, present and future happenings, and clairvoyance do not constitute wisdom-insight.

26. *What is the relation between desirelessness and wisdom?*

Desirelessness is wisdom. The two are not different; they are the same. Desirelessness is refraining from driving the mind toward any object. Wisdom means the appearance of no object. In other words, not seeking what is other than the

Self is detachment or desirelessness; not leaving the Self is wisdom.

27. *What is the difference between inquiry and meditation?*

Inquiry consists in retaining the mind in the Self. Meditation consists in thinking that one's self is *Brahman*, existence-consciousness-bliss.

28. *What is release?*

Inquiring into the nature of one's self that is in bondage and realizing one's true nature is release.

SPIRITUAL INSTRUCTION

Instruction
(Upadeśa)

1. *What are the marks of a real teacher (sadguru)?*

Steady abidance in the Self, looking at all with an equal eye, unshakable courage at all times, in all places and circumstances, etc.

2. *What are the marks of an earnest disciple* (sadśiṣya)?

An intense longing for the removal of sorrow and attainment of joy, and an intense aversion for all kinds of mundane pleasure.

3. *What are the characteristics of instruction* (upadeśa)?

The word *upadeśa* means "near the place or seat" (*upa,* near; *deśa,* place or seat). The Guru, who is the embodiment of that which is indicated by the terms *sat, chit* and *ānanda* (existence, consciousness and bliss), prevents the disciple who, on account of his acceptance of the forms of the objects of the senses, has swerved from his true state and is consequently distressed and buffeted by joys and sorrows, from continuing so and establishes him in his own real nature without differentiation.

Upadeśa also means showing a distant object quite near. It is brought home to the disciple that *Brahman,* which he believes to be distant and different from himself, is near and not different from himself.

4. *If it be true that the Guru is one's own Self* (ātman), *what is the principle underlying the doctrine which says that, however learned a disciple may be or whatever occult pow-*

ers he may possess, he cannot attain self-realization (ātma-siddhi) *without the grace of the Guru?*

Although in absolute truth the state of the Guru is that of oneself, it is very hard for the Self which has become the individual soul (*jīva*) through ignorance to realize its true state or nature without the grace of the Guru.

All mental concepts are controlled by the mere presence of the real Guru. If he were to say to one who arrogantly claims that he has seen the further shore of the ocean of learning or one who claims arrogantly that he can perform deeds which are well nigh impossible, "Yes, you learned all that is to be learned, but have you learned (to know) yourself? And you who are capable of performing deeds which are almost impossible, have you seen yourself?," they will bow their heads (in shame) and remain silent. Thus it is evident that only by the grace of the Guru and by no other accomplishment is it possible to know oneself.

5. *What are the marks of the Guru's grace?*

It is beyond words or thoughts.

6. *If that is so, how is it that it is said that the disciple realizes his true state by the Guru's grace?*

It is like the elephant which wakes up on seeing a lion in its dream. Even as the elephant wakes up at the mere sight of the lion, so too is it certain that the disciple wakes up from the sleep of ignorance into the wakefulness of true knowledge through the Guru's benevolent look of grace.

7. *What is the significance of the saying that the nature of the real Guru is that of the Supreme Lord (Sarveśvara)?*

In the case of the individual soul which desires to attain the state of true knowledge or the state of Godhood (Īśvara) and with that object always practices devotion, the Lord, who is the witness of that individual soul and identical with it, comes forth, when the individual's devotion has reached a mature stage, in human form with the help of *sat-chit-ānanda,* His three natural features and form and name which he also graciously assumes, and in the guise of blessing the disciple, absorbs him in Himself. According to this doctrine the Guru can truly be called the Lord.

8. *How, then, did some great persons attain knowledge without a Guru?*

To a few mature persons the Lord shines as the light of knowledge and imparts awareness of the truth.

9. *What is the end of devotion* (bhakti) *and the path of Siddhānta (i.e., Śaiva Siddhānta)?*

It is to learn the truth that all one's actions performed with unselfish devotion, with the aid of the three purified instruments (body, speech, and mind), in the capacity of the servant of the Lord, become the Lord's actions, and to stand forth free from the sense of "I" and "mine." This is also the truth of what the Śaiva-Siddhāntins call *parā-bhakti* (supreme devotion) or living in the service of God (*irai-pani-nittal*).

10. *What is the end of the path of knowledge* (jnana) *or Vedānta?*

It is to know the truth that the "I" is not different from the Lord (Īśvara) and to be free from the feeling of being the doer (*kartṛtva, ahaṃkāra*).

11. *How can it be said that the end of both these paths is the same?*

Whatever the means, the destruction of the sense of "I" and "mine" is the goal, and as these are interdependent, the destruction of either of them causes the destruction of the other; therefore, in order to achieve that state of Silence which is beyond thought and word, either the path of knowledge which removes the sense of "I" or the path of devotion which removes the sense of "mine" will suffice. So there is no doubt that the end of the paths of devotion and knowledge is one and the same.

Note: So long as the "I" exists, it is necessary to accept the Lord also. If anyone wishes to regain easily the supreme state of identity (*sāyujya*) now lost to him, it is only proper that he should accept this conclusion.

12. *What is the mark of the ego?*

The individual soul of the form of "I" is the ego. The Self which is of the nature of intelligence (*chit*) has no sense of "I." Nor does the insentient body possess a sense of "I." The mysterious appearance of a delusive ego between the intelligent and the insentient being the root cause of all these troubles, upon its destruction by whatever means, that which really exists will be seen as it is. This is called Liberation (*mokṣa*).

Practice

(ABHYĀSA)

1. *What is the method of practice?*

As the Self of a person who tries to attain Self-realization is not different from him and as there is nothing other than or superior to him to be attained by him, Self-realization being only the realization of one's own nature, the seeker of Liberation realizes, without doubts or misconceptions, his real nature by distinguishing the eternal from the transient, and never swerves from his natural state. This is known as the practice of knowledge. This is the inquiry leading to Self-realization.

2. *Can this path of inquiry be followed by all aspirants?*

This is suitable only for the ripe souls. The rest should follow different methods according to the state of their minds.

3. *What are the other methods?*

They are (a) *stuti*, (b) *japa*, (c) *dhyāna*, (d) *yoga*, (e) *jnāna*, and so forth.

(a) *Stuti* is singing the praises of the Lord with a great feeling of devotion.

(b) *Japa* is uttering the names of the gods or sacred *mantras* like *om* either mentally or verbally.

(While following the methods of *stuti* and *japa* the mind will sometimes be concentrated [lit. closed] and sometimes diffused [lit. open], The vagaries of the mind will not be evident to those who follow these methods.)

(c) *Dhyāna* denotes the repetition of the names, etc., mentally (*japa*) with feelings of devotion. In this method the state of the mind will be understood easily. For the mind does not become concentrated and diffused simultaneously. When one is in *dhyāna* it does not contact the objects of the senses, and when it is in contact with the objects it is not in *dhyāna*. Therefore those who are in this state can observe the vagaries of the mind then and there and, by stopping the mind from thinking other thoughts, fix it in *dhyāna*. Perfection in *dhyāna* is the state of abiding in the Self (lit. abiding in the form of "that," *tadākāranilai*).

As meditation functions in an exceedingly subtle manner at the source of the mind, it is not difficult to perceive its rise and subsidence.

(d) *Yoga:* The source of the breath is the same as that of the mind; therefore the subsidence of either leads effortlessly to that of the other. The practice of stilling the mind through breath control (*praṇayāma*) is called yoga.

Fixing their minds on psychic centers such as the *sahasrāra* (lit. the thousand-petaled lotus), yogis remain any length of time without awareness of their bodies. As long as this state continues they appear to be immersed in some kind of joy. But when the mind which has become tranquil emerges (becomes active again), it resumes its worldly thoughts. It is therefore necessary to train it with the help of practices like *dhyāna* whenever it becomes externalized. It will then attain a state in which there is neither subsidence nor emergence.

(e) *Jñāna* is the annihilation of the mind in which it is made to assume the form of the Self through the constant practice of *dhyāna* or inquiry (*vichāra*). The extinction of the mind is the state in which there is a cessation of all efforts. Those who are established in this state never swerve from their true state. The terms *silence* (*mouna*) and *inaction* refer to this state alone.

NOTE: (1) All practices are followed only with the object of concentrating the mind. As all the mental activities like remembering, forgetting, desiring, hating, attracting, discarding, etc., are modifications of the mind, they cannot be one's true state. Simple, changeless being is one's true nature. Therefore, to know the truth of one's being and to *be* it is known as release from bondage and the destruction of the knot (*granthi nāśam*). Until this state of tranquillity of mind is firmly attained, the practice of unswerving abidance in the Self and keeping the mind unsoiled by various thoughts is essential for an aspirant.

(2) Although the practices for achieving strength of mind are numerous, all of them achieve the same end. For it can be seen that whoever concentrates his mind on any object will, on the cessation of all mental concepts, ultimately remain merely as that object. This is called successful meditation (*dhyāna siddhi*). Those who follow the path of inquiry realize that the mind which remains at the end of the inquiry is *Brahman*. Those who practice meditation realize that the mind which remains at the end of the meditation is the object of their meditation. As the result is the same in either case, it is the duty of aspirants to practice continuously either of these methods till the goal is reached.

4. *Is the state of being still a state involving effort or effortless?*

It is not an effortless state of indolence. All mundane activities which are ordinarily called effort are performed with the aid of a portion of the mind and with frequent breaks. But the act of communion with the Self (*ātma vyavahāra*) or remaining still inwardly is intense activity which is performed with the entire mind and without break.

5. *What is the nature of* māyā*?*

Māyā is that which makes us regard as nonexistent the Self, the Reality, which is always and everywhere present and all-pervasive and self-luminous, and as existent the individual soul (*jīva*), the world (*jagat*), and God (*para*), which have been conclusively proved to be nonexistent at all times and places.

6. *As the Self shines fully of its own accord, why is it not generally recognized like the other objects of the world by all persons?*

Wherever particular objects are known, it is the Self which has known itself in the form of those objects. For what is known as knowledge or awareness is only the potency of the Self (*ātma śakti*). The Self is the only sentient object. There is nothing apart from the Self. If there are such objects, they are all insentient and therefore cannot either know themselves or mutually know one another. It is because the Self does not know its true nature in this manner that it seems to be immersed and struggling in the ocean of birth (or death) in the form of the individual soul.

7. *Although the Lord is all-pervasive, it appears, from passages like "adorning Him through His Grace," that He can be known only through His grace. How, then, can the individual soul by its own efforts attain self-realization in the absence of the Lord's Grace?*

As the Lord denotes the Self and as Grace means the Lord's presence or revelation, there is no time when the Lord remains unknown. If the light of the sun is invisible to the owl, it is only the fault of that bird and not of the sun. Similarly, can the unawareness by ignorant persons of the Self, which is always of the nature of awareness, be other than their own fault? How can it be the fault of the Self? It is because Grace is of the very nature of the Lord that He is well known as "the blessed Grace." Therefore, the Lord, whose nature itself is Grace, does not have to bestow His Grace. Nor is there any particular time for bestowing His Grace.

8. *What part of the body is the abode of the Self?*

The heart on the right side of the chest is generally indicated. This is because we usually point to the right side of the chest when we refer to ourselves. Some say that the *sahasrāra* (the thousand-petaled lotus) is the abode of the Self.

But if that were true, the head should not fall forward when we go to sleep or faint.

9. *What is the nature of the heart?*

The sacred texts describing it say: Between the two nipples, below the chest and above the abdomen, there are six organs of different colors.[1] One of them resembling the bud of a water lily and situated two digits to the right is the heart. It is inverted and within it is a tiny orifice which is the seat of dense darkness (ignorance) full of desires. All the psychic nerves (*nāḍīs*) depend upon it. It is the abode of the vital forces, the mind and the light (of consciousness).

But, although it is described thus, the meaning of the word *heart* (*hṛdayam*) is the Self (*Ātman*). As it is denoted by the terms *existence, consciousness, bliss, eternal,* and *plenum* (*sat, chit, ānandam, nityam, pūrṇam*) it has no differences such as exterior and interior or up and down. That tranquil state in which all thoughts come to an end is called the state of the Self. When it is realized as it is, there is no scope for discussions about its location inside the body or outside.

10. *Why do thoughts of many objects arise in the mind even when there is no contact with external objects?*

All such thoughts are due to latent tendencies (*pūrva saṃskāras*). They appear only to the individual consciousness (*jīva*) which has forgotten its real nature and become externalized. Whenever particular things are perceived, the inquiry "Who is it that sees them?" should be made; they will then disappear at once.

11. *How do the triple factors (knower, known, and knowledge), which are absent in deep sleep,* samādhi, *etc., manifest themselves in the Self (in the states of waking and dreaming)?*

From the self there arise in succession

(a) *chidābhāsa* (reflected consciousness), which is a kind of luminosity

(b) *jīva* (the individual consciousness) or the seer or the first concept

(c) phenomena, that is, the world

12. *Since the Self is free from the notions of knowledge and ignorance, how can it be said to pervade the entire body in the shape of sentience or to impart sentience to the senses?*

Wise men say that there is a connection between the source of the various psychic nerves and the Self, that this is the knot of the heart, that the connection between the sentient and the insentient will exist until this is cut asunder with the aid of true knowledge, that just as the suble and invisible force of electricity travels through wires and does many wonderful things, so the force of the Self also travels through the psychic nerves and, pervading the entire body, imparts sentience to the senses, and that if this knot is cut the Self will remain as it always is, without any attributes.

13. *How can there be a connection between the Self, which is pure knowledge, and the triple factors, which are relative knowledge?*

This is, in a way, like the working of a cinema as shown in the accompanying chart.

Just as the pictures appear on the screen as long as the film throws the shadows through the lens, so the phenomenal world will continue to appear to the individual in the waking and dream states as long as there are latent mental impressions. Just as the lens magnifies the tiny specks on the film to a huge size and as a number of pictures are shown in a second, so the mind enlarges the sproutlike tendencies into treelike thoughts and shows in a second innumerable worlds. Again, just as there is only the light of the lamp visible when there is no film, so the Self alone shines without the triple factors when the mental concepts in the form of tendencies are absent in the states of deep sleep, swoon, and *samādhi*. Just as the lamp illuminates the lens, etc., while remaining

Cinema Show	Self
a. The lamp inside (the apparatus)	a. The Self
b. The lens in front of the lamp	b. The pure (sattvic) mind close to the Self
c. The film, which is a long series of separate photos	c. The stream of latent tendencies consisting of subtle thoughts
d. The lens, the light passing through it, and the lamp, which together form the focused light	d. The mind, the illumination of it, and the Self, which together form the seer or the *jīva*
e. The light passing through the lens and falling on the screen	e. The light of the Self emerging from the mind through the senses and falling on the world
f. The various kinds of pictures appearing in the light of the screen	f. The various forms and names appearing as the objects perceived in the light of the world
g. The mechanism which sets the film in motion	g. The divine law manifesting the latent tendencies of the mind

unaffected, the Self illumines the ego (*chidābhāsa*), etc., while remaining unaffected.

14. *What is dhyāna (meditation)?*

It is abiding as one's Self without swerving in any way from one's real nature and without feeling that one is meditating. As one is not in the least conscious of the different states (waking, dreaming, etc.) in this condition, the sleep (noticeable) here is also regarded as *dhyāna*.

15. *What is the difference between dhyāna and samādhi?*

Dhyāna is achieved through deliberate mental effort; in *samādhi* there is no such effort.

16. *What are the factors to be kept in view in dhyāna?*

It is important for one who is established in his Self (*ātma niṣṭha*) to see that he does not swerve in the least from this absorption. By swerving from his true nature he may see before him bright effulgences, etc., or hear (unusual) sounds or regard as real the visions of gods appearing within or outside himself. He should not be deceived by these and forget himself.

NOTE: (1) If the moments that are wasted in thinking of the objects which are not the Self are spent on inquiry into the Self, Self-realization will be attained in a very short time.

(2) Until the mind becomes established in itself, some kind of *bhāvanā* (contemplation of a personified god or goddess with deep emotion and religious feeling) is essential. Otherwise the mind will be frequently assailed by wayward thoughts or sleep.

(3) Without spending all the time in practicing *bhāvanās* like "I am Shiva" or "I am *Brahman*," which are regarded as *nirguṇopāsana* (contemplation of the attributeless Brahman), the method of inquiry into oneself should be practiced as soon as the mental strength which is the result of such *upāsana* (contemplation) is attained.

(4) The excellence of the practice (*sādhana*) lies in not giving room for even a single mental concept (*vṛtti*).

17. *What are the rules of conduct which an aspirant (*sādhaka*) should follow?*

Moderation in food, moderation in sleep, and moderation in speech.

18. *How long should one practice?*

Until the mind attains effortlessly its natural state of freedom from concepts, that is, till the sense of "I" and "mine" exists no longer.

19. *What is the meaning of dwelling in solitude* (ekānta vāsa)?

As the Self is all-pervasive, it has no particular place for solitude. The state of being free from mental concepts is called dwelling in solitude.

20. *What is the sign of wisdom* (vīveka)?

Its beauty lies in remaining free from delusion after realizing the truth once. There is fear only for one who sees at least a slight difference in the Supreme *Brahman.* So long as there is the idea that the body is the Self, one cannot be a realizer of truth, whoever he might be.

21. *If everything happens according to karma* (prārabdha: *the result of one's acts in the past), how is one to overcome the obstacles to meditation* (dhyāna)?

Prārabdha concerns only the out-turned, not the in-turned mind. One who seeks his real Self will not be afraid of any obstacle.

22. *Is asceticism* (sannyāsa) *one of the essential requisites for a person to become established in the Self* (ātma niṣṭha)?

The effort that is made to get rid of attachment to one's body is really toward abiding in the Self. Maturity of thought and inquiry alone removes attachment to the body, not the stations of life (*āśramas*), such as student (*brahmachāri*), etc. For the attachment is in the mind while the stations pertain to the body. How can bodily stations remove the attachment in the mind? As maturity of thought and inquiry pertain to the mind, these alone can, by inquiry on the part of the same mind, remove the attachments which have crept into it through thoughtlessness. But, as the discipline of asceticism (*sannyasāśrama*) is the means for attaining dispassion (*vairāgya*), and as dispassion is the means for inquiry, joining an order of ascetics may be regarded, in a way, as a means of inquiry through dispassion. Instead of wasting one's life by entering the order of ascetics before one is fit for it, it is better to live the householder's life. In order to fix the mind in the Self, which is its true nature, it is necessary to separate it from the family of fancies (*saṃkalpas*) and doubts (*vikalpas*), that is, to renounce the family (*saṃsāra*) in the mind. This is the real asceticism.

23. *It is an established rule that so long as there is the least idea of I-am-the-doer, Self-knowledge cannot be attained, but is it possible for an aspirant who is a householder to discharge his duties properly without this sense?*

As there is no rule that action should depend upon a sense of being the doer, it is unnecessary to doubt whether any action will take place without a doer or an act of doing. Although the officer of a government treasury may appear, in the eyes of others, to be doing his duty attentively and responsibly all day long, he will be discharging his duties without attachment, thinking, "I have no real connection with all this money" and without a sense of involvement in his mind. In the same manner a wise householder may also discharge without attachment the various household duties which fall to his lot according to his past karma, like a tool in the hands of another. Action and knowledge are not obstacles to each other.

24. *Of what use to his family is a wise householder who is unmindful of his bodily comforts, and of what use is his family to him?*

Although he is entirely unmindful of his bodily comforts, if, owing to his past karma, his family has to subsist by his efforts, he may be regarded as doing service to others. If it is asked whether the wise man derives any benefit from the discharge of domestic duties, it may be answered that, as he has already attained the state of complete satisfaction which is the sum total of all benefits and the highest good of all, he does not stand to gain anything more by discharging family duties.

25. *How can cessation of activity (*nivṛtti*) and peace of mind be attained in the midst of household duties, which are of the nature of constant activity?*

As the activities of the wise man exist only in the eyes of others and not in his own, although he may be accomplishing immense tasks, he really does nothing. Therefore, his activities do not stand in the way of inaction and peace of mind. For he knows the truth that all activities take place in his mere presence and that he does nothing. Hence he will remain as the silent witness of all the activities taking place.

26. *Just as the Sage's past karma is the cause of his present activities, will not the impressions (*vāsanās*) caused by his present activities adhere to him in future?*

Only one who is free from all the latent tendencies (*vāsanas*) is a Sage. That being so, how can the tendencies of karma affect him who is entirely unattached to activity?

27. *What is the meaning of* brahmacharya*?*

Only inquiry into *Brahman* should be called *brahmacharya.*

28. *Will the practice of* brahmacharya *which is followed in conformity with the (four) orders of life (*āśramas*) be a means of knowledge?*

As the various means of knowledge, such as control of senses, etc., are included in *brahmacharya,* the virtuous practices duly followed by those who belong to the order of students (*brahmachārins*) are very helpful for their improvement.

29. *Can one enter the order of ascetics* (sannyāsa) *directly from the order of students* (brahmacharya)*?*

Those who are competent need not formally enter the orders of *brahmacharya,* etc., in the order laid down. One who has realized his Self does not distinguish between the various orders of life. Therefore, no order of life either helps or hinders him.

30. *Does an aspirant* (sādhaka) *lose anything by not observing the rules of caste and orders of life?*

As the attainment (*anuṣṭhāna,* lit. practice) of knowledge is the supreme end of all other practices, there is no rule that one who remains in any one order of life and constantly acquires knowledge is bound to follow the rules laid down for that order of life. If he follows the rules of caste and orders of life, he does so for the good of the world. He does not derive any benefit by observing the rules. Nor does he lose anything by not observing them.

Experience
(ANUBHAVA)

1. *What is the light of consciousness?*

It is the self-luminous existence-consciousness which reveals to the seer the world of names and forms both inside and outside. The existence of this existence-consciousness can be inferred by the objects illuminated by it. It does not become the object of consciousness.

2. *What is knowledge (*vijñāna*)?*

It is that tranquil state of existence-consciousness which is experienced by the aspirant and which is like the waveless ocean or the motionless ether.

3. *What is bliss?*

It is the experience of joy (or peace) in the state of *vijñāna* free of all activities and similar to deep sleep. This is also called the state of *kevala nirvikalpa* (remaining without concepts).

4. *What is the state beyond bliss?*

It is the state of unceasing peace of mind which is found in the state of absolute quiescence, *jagrat-suṣupti* (lit. sleep with awareness), which resembles inactive deep sleep. In this state, in spite of the activity of the body and the senses, there is no external awareness, as in the case of a child immersed in sleep[2] (who is not conscious of the food given to him by his mother). A yogi who is in this state is inactive even while engaged in activity. This is also called *sahaja-nirvikalpa samādhi* (natural state of absorption in oneself without concepts).

5. *What is the authority for saying that the entire moving and unmoving worlds depend upon oneself?*

The Self means the embodied being. It is only after the energy, which was latent in the state of deep sleep, emerges with the idea of "I" that all objects are experienced. The Self is present in all perceptions as the perceiver. There are no objects to be seen when the "I" is absent. For all these reasons it may undoubtedly be said that everything comes out of the Self and goes back to the Self.

6. *As the bodies and the selves animating them are everywhere actually observed to be innumerable, how can it be said that the Self is only one?*

If the idea "I am the body" is accepted,[3] the selves are multiple. The state in which this idea vanishes is the Self since in that state there are no other objects. It is for this reason that the Self is regarded as one only.

7. *What is the authority for saying that* Brahman *can be apprehended by the mind and at the same time that it cannot be apprehended by the mind?*

It cannot be apprehended by the impure mind but can be apprehended by the pure mind.

8. *What is pure mind and what is impure mind?*

When the indefinable power of *Brahman* separates itself from *Brahman* and, in union with the reflection of consciousness (*chidābhāsa*), assumes various forms, it is called the impure mind. When it becomes free from the reflection of consciousness (*ābhāsa*), through discrimination, it is called the pure mind. Its state of union with the *Brahman* is its apprehension of *Brahman.* The energy which is accompanied by the reflection of consciousness is called the impure mind, and its state of separation from *Brahman* is its nonapprehension of *Brahman.*

9. *Is it possible to overcome, even while the body exists, the karma* (prārabdha) *which is said to last till the end of the body?*

Yes. If the agent (doer) upon whom the karma depends, namely the ego, which has come into existence between the body and the Self, merges in its source and loses its form, will the karma which depends upon it alone survive? Therefore when there is no "I" there is no karma.

10. *As the Self is existence and consciousness, what is the reason for describing it as different from the existent and the nonexistent, the sentient and the insentient?*

Although the Self is real, as it comprises everything, it does not give room for questions involving duality about its reality or unreality. Therefore it is said to be different from the real and the unreal. Similarly, even though it is consciousness, since there is nothing for it to know or to make itself known to, it is said to be different from the sentient and the insentient.

Attainment
(Ārudha)

1. *What is the state of attainment of knowledge?*

It is firm and effortless abidance in the Self in which the mind which has become one with the Self does not subsequently emerge again at any time. That is, just as everyone usually and naturally has the idea "I am not a goat nor a cow nor any other animal but a man," when he thinks of his body, so also when he has the idea "I am not the principles (*tattvas*) beginning with the body and ending with sound (*nāda*), but the Self which is existence, consciousness, and bliss," the innate self-consciousness (*ātma prajña*), he is said to have attained firm knowledge.

2. *To which of the seven stages of knowledge (*jñāna-bhūmikas*)*[4] *does the sage (*jñāni*) belong?*

He belongs to the fourth stage.

3. *If that is so, why have three more stages superior to it been distinguished?*

The marks of the stages four to seven are based upon the experiences of the realized person (*jīvanmukta*). They are not states of knowledge and release. So far as knowledge and release are concerned, no distinction whatever is made in these four stages.

4. *As liberation is common to all, why is the* variṣṭha *(lit. the most excellent) alone praised excessively?*

So far as the *variṣṭha*'s common experience of bliss is concerned, he is extolled only because of the special merit acquired by him in his previous births, which is the cause of it.

5. *As there is no one who does not desire to experience constant bliss, what is the reason why all sages (*jñānis*) do not attain the state of* variṣṭha*?*

It is not to be attained by mere desire or effort. Karma (*prārabdha*) is its cause. As the ego dies along with its cause even in the fourth stage (*bhūmika*), what agent is there beyond that stage to desire anything or to make efforts? So long as they make efforts they will not be sages (*jñānis*). Do the sacred texts (*śrutis*) which specially mention the *variṣṭha* say that the other three are unenlightened persons?

6. *As some sacred texts say that the supreme state is that in which the sense organs and the mind are completely destroyed, how can that state be compatible with the experience of the body and the senses?*

If that were so there would not be any difference between that state and the state of deep sleep. Further, how can it be said to be the natural state when it exists at one time and not at another? This happens, as stated before, to some persons according to their karma (*prārabdha*) for some time or till death. It cannot properly be regarded as the final state. If it could, it would mean that all great souls and the Lord, who were the authors of the Vedantic works (*jñāna granthas*) and the Vedas, were unenlightened persons. If the supreme state is that in which neither the senses nor the mind exists and not the state in which they exist, how can it be the perfect state (*paripurṇam*)? As karma alone is responsible for the activity or inactivity of the sages, great souls have declared the state of *sahaja-nirvikalpa* (the natural state without concepts) alone to be the ultimate state.

7. *What is the difference between ordinary sleep and waking sleep (*jāgrat suṣupti*)?*

In ordinary sleep there are not only no thoughts but also no awareness. In waking sleep there is awareness alone. That is why it is called awake while sleeping, that is, the sleep in which there is awareness.

8. *Why is the Self described both as the fourth state (*turīya*) and beyond the fourth state (*turīyātita*)?*

Turīya means that which is the fourth. The experiencers (*jīvas*) of the three states of waking, dreaming, and deep sleep, known as *viśva, taijasa,* and *prajñā,*[5] who wander successively in these three states, are not the Self. It is with the object of making this clear, namely that the Self is that which is different from them and which is the witness of these states, that it is called the fourth (*turīya*). When this is known, the three experiencers disappear and the idea that the Self is a witness, that it is the fourth, also disappears. That is why the Self is described as beyond the fourth (*turīyātita*).

9. *What is the benefit derived by the sage from the sacred books (*sruṭis*)?*

The sage who is the embodiment of the truths mentioned in the scriptures has no use for them.

10. *Is there any connection between the attainment of supernatural powers (*siddhis*) and Liberation (*mukti*)?*

Enlightened inquiry alone leads to Liberation. Supernatural powers are all illusory appearances created by the power of *māyā* (*māyāśakti*). Self-realization which is permanent is the only true accomplishment (*siddhi*). Accomplishments which appear and disappear, being the effect of *māyā,* cannot be real. They are accomplished with the object of enjoying fame, pleasures, etc. They come unsought to some persons through their karma. Know that union with *Brahman* is the real aim of all accomplishments. This is also the state of Liberation (*aikya mukti*) known as union (*sāyujya*).

11. *If this is the nature of liberation (*mokṣa*), why do some scriptures connect it with the body and say that the individual soul can attain liberation only when it does not leave the body?*

It is only if bondage is real that liberation and the nature of its experiences have to be considered. So far as the Self (*puruṣa*) is concerned, it has really no bondage in any of the four states. As bondage is merely a verbal assumption according to the emphatic proclamation of the Vedānta system, how can the question of liberation, which depends upon the question of bondage, arise when there is no bondage? Without knowing this truth, to inquire into the nature of bondage and liberation, is like inquiring into the nonexistent height, color, etc., of a barren woman's son or the horns of a hare.

12. *If that is so, do not the descriptions of bondage and release found in the scriptures become irrelevant and untrue?*

No, they do not. On the contrary, the delusion of bondage fabricated by ignorance from time immemorial can be removed only by knowledge, and for this purpose the term *liberation* (*mukti*) has been usually accepted. That is all. The fact that the characteristics of liberation are described in different ways proves that they are imaginary.

13. *If that is so, are not all efforts such as study (lit. hearing) and reflection useless?*

No, they are not. The firm conviction that there is neither bondage nor liberation is the supreme purpose of all efforts. As this purpose of seeing boldly, through direct experience, that bondage and liberation do not exist, cannot be achieved except with the aid of the aforesaid practices, these efforts are useful.

14. *Is there any authority for saying that there is neither bondage nor liberation?*

This is decided on the strength of experience and not merely on the strength of the scriptures.

15. *If it is experienced, how is it experienced?*

Bondage and *liberation* are mere linguistic terms. They have no reality of their own. Therefore they cannot function of their own accord. It is necessary to accept the existence of some basic thing of which they are the modifications. If one inquires, "For whom is there bondage and liberation?" it will be seen, "They are for me." If one inquires, "Who am I?," one will see that there is no such thing as the "I." It will then be as clear as an *āmalaka* fruit in one's hand that what remains is one's real being. As this truth will be naturally and clearly experienced by those who leave aside mere verbal discussions and inquire into themselves inwardly, there is no doubt that all realized persons uniformly see neither bondage nor liberation so far as the true Self is concerned.

16. *If truly there is neither bondage nor liberation, what is the reason for the actual experience of joys and sorrows?*

They appear to be real only when one turns aside from one's real nature. They do not really exist.

17. *Is it possible for everyone to know directly without doubt what exactly is one's true nature?*

Undoubtedly it is possible.

18. *How?*

It is the experience of everyone that even in the states of deep sleep, fainting, etc., when the entire universe, moving and stationary, beginning with earth and ending with the unmanifested (*prakṛti*), disappears, he does not disappear. Therefore the state of pure being which is common to all and which is always experienced directly by everybody is one's true nature. The conclusion is that all experiences in the enlightened as well as the ignorant state, which may be described by newer and newer words, are opposed to one's real nature.

MAHARSHI'S GOSPEL

Work and Renunciation

Disciple. What is the highest goal of spiritual experience for man?

Maharshi. Self-realization.

D. Can a married man realize the Self?

M. Certainly. Married or unmarried, a man can realize the Self, because That is here and now. If it were not so, but attainable by some effort at some time, and if it were new and had to be acquired, it would not be worth pursuit, because what is not natural is not permanent either. But what I say is that the Self is here and now, and alone.

D. A salt-doll diving into the sea will not be protected by a waterproof coat. This world in which we have to toil day in and day out is like the ocean.

M. Yes, the mind is the waterproof coat.

D. So, then, one may be engaged in work and, free from desire, keep up one's solitude? But life's duties allow little time to sit in meditation or even to pray.

M. Yes. Work performed with attachment is a shackle, whereas work performed with detachment does not affect the doer. He is, even while working, in solitude. To engage in your duty is the true *namaskār* . . . and abiding in God is the only true *asan.*

D. Should I not renounce my home?

M. If that had been your destiny the question would not have arisen.

D. Why then did you leave your home in your youth?

M. Nothing happens except by divine dispensation. One's course of conduct in this life is determined by one's *prārabdha*.

D. Is it good to devote all my time to the search for the Self? If that is impossible, should I merely keep quiet?

M. If you can keep quiet, without engaging in any other pursuit, it is very good. If that cannot be done, where is the use of being quiet so far as Realization is concerned? So long as a person is obliged to be active, let him not give up attempts to realize the Self.

D. Do not one's actions affect one in later births?

M. Are you born now? Why do you think of other births? The fact is, there is neither birth nor death. Let him who is born think of death and the palliative thereof!

D. Can you show us the dead?

M. Did you know your kinsmen before their birth that you should seek to know them after their death?

D. How does a *gṛhastha* fare in the scheme of *mokṣa*? Should he not necessarily become a mendicant in order to attain Liberation?

M. Why do you think you are a *gṛhastha*? Similar thoughts that you are a *sannyāsin* will haunt you, even if you go out as a *sannyāsin*. Whether you continue in the household or renounce it and go to the forest, your mind haunts you. The ego is the source of thought. It creates the body and the world, and it makes you think of being the *gṛhastha*. If you renounce, it will only substitute the thought of *sannyāsa* for that of *gṛhastha*, and the environment of the forest for that of the household. But the mental obstacles are always there for you. They even increase greatly in the new surroundings. It is no help to change the environment. The one obstacle is the mind; it must be got over whether in the home or in the forest. If you can do it in the forest, why not in the home? Therefore, why change the environment? Your efforts can be made even now, whatever be the environment.

D. Is it possible to enjoy *samādhi* while busy in worldly work?

M. The feeling "I work" is the hindrance. Ask yourself, "Who works?" Remember who you are. Then the work will not bind you; it will go on automatically. Make no effort either to work or to renounce; your effort is the bondage. What is destined to happen will happen. If you are destined not to work, work cannot be had even if you hunt for it; if you are destined to work, you will not be able to avoid it; you will be forced to engage yourself in it. So leave it to the Higher Power; you cannot renounce or retain as you choose.

D. Bhagavan said yesterday that while one is engaged in search of God "within," "outer" work would go on automatically. In the life of Śrī Chaitanya it is said that during his lectures to students he was really seeking Krishna (Self) within, forgot all about his body, and went on talking of Krishna only. This raises a doubt whether work can safely be left to itself. Should one keep part-attention on the physical work?

M. The Self is all. Are you apart from the Self? Or can the work go on without the Self? The Self is universal; so all actions will go on whether you strain yourself to be engaged in them or not. The work will go on of itself. Thus Krishna told Arjuna that he need not trouble to kill the Kauravas; they were already slain by God. It was not for him to resolve to work and worry himself about it, but to allow his own nature to carry out the will of the Higher Power.

D. But the work may suffer if I do not attend to it.

M. Attending to the Self means attending to the work. Because you identify yourself with the body, you think that work is done by you. But the body and its activities, including that work, are not apart from the Self. What does it matter whether you attend to the work or not? Suppose you walk from one place to another: you do not attend to the steps you take. Yet you find yourself after a time at your goal. You see how the business of walking goes on without your attending to it. So also with other kinds of work.

D. It is then like sleepwalking.

M. Like somnambulism? Quite so. When a child is fast asleep, his mother feeds him; the child eats the food just as well as when he is fully awake. But the next morning he says to the mother, "Mother, I did not take food last night." The mother and others know that he did, but he says that he did not; he was not aware. Still the action had gone on.

A traveler in a cart has fallen asleep. The bulls move, stand still, or are unyoked during the journey. He does not know these events but finds himself in a different place after he wakes up. He has been blissfully ignorant of the occurrences on the way, but the journey has been finished. Similarly with the Self of a person. The ever-wakeful Self is compared to the traveler asleep in the cart. The waking state is the moving of the bulls; *samādhi* is their standing still (because *samādhi* means *jagratsuṣupti,* that is to say, the person is aware but not concerned in the action; the bulls are yoked but do not move); sleep is the unyoking of the bulls, for there is complete stopping of activity corresponding to the relief of the bulls from the yoke.

Or again, take the instance of the cinema. Scenes are projected on the screen in the cinema show. But the moving pictures do not affect or alter the screen. The spectator pays attention to them, not to the screen. They cannot exist apart from the screen, yet the screen is ignored. So also, the Self is the screen where the pictures, activities, etc., are seen going on. The man is aware of the latter but not aware of the essential former. All the same the world of pictures is not apart from the Self. Whether he is aware of the screen or unaware, the actions will continue.

D. But there is an operator in the cinema!

M. The cinema show is made out of insentient materials. The lamp, the pictures, the screen, etc., are all insentient and so they need an operator, the sentient agent. On the other hand, the Self is absolute Consciousness, and therefore self-contained. There cannot be an operator apart from the Self.

D. I am not confusing the body with the operator; rather, I am referring to Krishna's words in chapter 18, verse 61, of the *Gītā*: "The Lord, O Arjuna, dwells in the Heart of every being, and He by His delusive power spins round all beings set as if on a machine."

M. The functions of the body involving the need for an operator are borne in mind; since the body is *jada* or insentient, a sentient operator is necessary. Because people think that they are *jīvas*, Krishna said that God resides in the Heart as the Operator of the *jīvas*. In fact, there are no *jīvas* and no Operator, as it were, outside them; the Self comprises all. It is the screen, the pictures, the seer, the actors, the operator, the light, the theater, and all else. Your confounding the Self with the body and imagining yourself the actor is like the seer representing himself as an actor in the cinema show. Imagine the actor asking if he can enact a scene without the screen! Such is the case of the man who thinks of his actions apart from the Self.

D. On the other hand, it is like asking the spectator to act in the cinema picture. So we must learn sleep-waking!

M. Actions and states are according to one's point of view. A crow, an elephant, a snake, each makes use of one limb for two alternate purposes. With one eye the crow looks on either side; for the elephant the trunk serves the purpose of both a hand and a nose; and the serpent sees as well as hears with its eyes. Whether you say the crow has an eye or eyes, or refer to the trunk of the elephant as "hand" or "nose," or call the eyes of the serpent its ears, it means all the same. Similarly, in the case of the *jñāni*, sleep-waking or waking-sleep or dream-sleep or dreaming-wakefulness, are all much the same thing.

D. But we have to deal with a physical body in a physical, waking world! If we sleep while working is going on, or try to work while asleep, the work will go wrong.

M. Sleep is not ignorance, it is one's pure state; wakefulness is not knowledge, it is ignorance. There is full awareness in sleep and total ignorance in waking. Your real nature covers both and extends beyond. The Self is beyond both knowledge and ignorance. Sleep, dream, and waking states are only modes passing before the Self: they proceed whether you are aware of them or not. That is the state of the *jñāni*, in whom pass the states of *samādhi*, waking, dream, and deep sleep, like the bulls moving, standing, or being unyoked, while the passenger is asleep. These answers are from the point of view of the *ajñāni;* otherwise such questions would not arise.

D. Of course, they cannot arise for the Self. Who would be there to ask? But unfortunately I have not yet realized the Self!

M. That is just the obstacle in your way. You must get rid of the idea that you are an *ajñāni* and have yet to realize the Self. You *are* the Self. Was there ever a time when you were not aware of that Self?

D. So we must experiment in sleep-waking . . . or in day-dreaming?

M. (Laughs)

D. I maintain that the physical body of the man immersed in *samādhi* as a result of the unbroken "contemplation"[6] of the Self, may become motionless for that reason. It may be active or inactive. The mind established in such contemplation will not be affected by the movements of the body or the senses; nor is disturbance of the mind the forerunner of physical activity. Whereas another person asserts that physical activity certainly prevents *samādhi* or unbroken contemplation. What is Bhagavan's opinion? You are the abiding proof of my statement.

M. Both of you are right: you refer to *sahaja nirvikalpa samādhi* and the other refers to *kevala nirvikalpa samādhi*. In the latter case the mind lies immersed in the Light of the Self (whereas the mind lies in the darkness of ignorance in deep sleep); and the subject makes a distinction between *samādhi* and activity after waking up from *samādhi*. Moreover, activity of the body, of the sight, of the vital forces, and of the mind and the cognizance of objects, all these are obstructions for one who seeks to realize *kevala nirvikalpa samādhi*.

In *sahaja samādhi*, however, the mind has resolved into the Self and has been lost. The differences and obstructions mentioned above do not, therefore, exist here. The activities of such a Being are like the feeding of a somnolent boy, perceptible to the onlooker but not to the subject. The traveler sleeping in the moving cart is not aware of the motion of the cart, because his mind is sunk in darkness; whereas the *sahaja jñāni* remains unaware of his bodily activities because his mind is dead, having been resolved into the ecstasy of *chidānanda* (bliss of the Self).[7]

Silence and Solitude

D. Is a vow of silence useful?

M. The inner silence is self-surrender. And that is living without the sense of ego.

D. Is solitude necessary for a *sannyāsin?*

M. Solitude is in the mind of a man. One might be in the thick of the world and yet maintain perfect serenity of mind; such a person is always in solitude. Another may stay in the forest but still be unable to control his mind. He cannot be said to be in solitude. Solitude is an attitude of the mind; a man attached to the things of life cannot get solitude, wherever he may be. A detached man is always in solitude.

D. What is *mouna*?

M. That state which transcends speech and thought is *mouna;* it is meditation without mental activity. Subjugation of the mind is meditation: deep meditation is eternal speech. Silence is ever-speaking; it is the perennial flow of "language." It is interrupted by speaking; for words obstruct this mute language. Lectures may entertain individuals for hours without improving them. Silence, on the other hand, is permanent and benefits the whole of humanity. . . . By silence, eloquence is meant. Oral lectures are not so eloquent as silence. Silence is unceasing eloquence. It is the best language. There is a state when words cease and silence prevails.

D. How then can we communicate our thoughts to one another?

M. That becomes necessary if the sense of duality exists.

D. Why does not Bhagavan go about and preach the Truth to the people at large?

M. How do you know I am not doing it? Does preaching consist in mounting a platform and haranguing the people around? Preaching is simple communication of Knowledge; it can really be done in silence only. What do you think of a man who listens to a sermon for an hour and goes away without having been impressed by it so as to change his life? Compare him with another who sits in a holy presence and goes away after some time with his outlook on life totally changed. Which is the better, to preach loudly without effect or to sit silently sending out inner force?

Again, how does speech arise? There is abstract Knowledge, whence arises the ego, which in turn gives rise to thought, and thought to the spoken word. So the word is the great-grandson of the original Source. If the word can produce effect, judge for yourself, how much more powerful must be the Preaching through Silence! But people do not understand this simple, bare truth, the Truth of their everyday, ever-present, eternal experience. This Truth is that of the Self. Is there anyone unaware of the Self? But they do not like even to hear of this Truth, whereas they are eager to know what lies beyond, about heaven, hell, and reincarnation.

Because they love mystery and not the Truth, religions cater to them so as eventually to bring them round to the Self. Whatever the means adopted, you must at last return to the Self: so why not abide in the Self here and now? To be a spectator of, or to speculate about, the other world, the Self is necessary; therefore, they are not different from the Self. Even the ignorant man, when he sees the objects, sees only the Self.

Mind Control

D. How can I control the mind?

M. There is no mind to control if the Self is realized. The Self shines forth when the mind vanishes. In the realized man the mind may be active or inactive; the Self alone exists. For the mind, body, and world are not separate from the Self; and they cannot remain apart from the Self. Can they be other than the Self? When aware of the Self, why should one worry about these shadows? How do they affect the Self?

D. If the mind is merely a shadow, how then is one to know the Self?

M. The Self is the Heart, self-luminous. Illumination arises from the Heart and reaches the brain, which is the seat of the mind. The world is seen with the mind; so you see the world by the reflected light of the Self. The world is perceived by an act of the mind. When the mind is illumined, it is aware of the world; when it is not so illumined, it is not aware of the world.

If the mind is turned in, toward the Source of illumination, objective knowledge ceases and the Self alone shines as the Heart.

The moon shines by reflecting the light of the sun. When the sun has set, the moon is useful for displaying objects. When the sun has risen, no one needs the moon, though its disc is visible in the sky. So it is with the mind and the Heart. The mind is made useful by its reflected light. It is used for seeing objects. When turned inward, it merges into the Source of illumination, which shines by Itself, and the mind is then like the moon in the daytime.

When it is dark, a lamp is necessary to give light. But when the sun has risen, there is no need for the lamp; the objects are visible. And to see the sun no lamp is necessary; it is enough if you turn your eyes toward the self-luminous sun. Similarly with the mind: to see the objects, the light reflected from the mind is necessary. To see the Heart, it is enough that the mind is turned toward it. Then the mind does not count and the Heart is self-effulgent.

D. After leaving this *āśrama,* in October, I was aware of the Presence that prevails in Śrī Bhagavan's Presence enfolding me for about ten days. All the time, while busy in my work, there was an undercurrent of that peace in unity; it was almost like the dual consciousness which one experiences while half-asleep during a dull lecture. Then, it faded out entirely; and the old stupidities came in instead. Work leaves no time for separate meditation. Is it enough constantly reminding oneself "I am," while at work?

M. (After a short pause) If you strengthen the mind, that peace will continue for all time. Its duration is proportional to the strength of mind acquired by repeated practice. And such a mind is able to hold on to the current. In that case, engagement or no engagement in work, the current remains unaffected and uninterrupted. It is not the work that hinders but the idea that it is *you* who are doing it.

D. Is a set meditation necessary for strengthening the mind?

M. Not if you keep the idea always before you that it is not your work. At first, effort is needed to remind yourself of it, but later on it becomes natural and continuous. The work will go on of its own accord, and your peace will remain undisturbed.

Meditation is your true nature. You call it meditation now, because there are other thoughts distracting you.

When these thoughts are dispelled, you remain alone—that is, in the state of meditation, free from thoughts; and that is your real nature, which you are now trying to gain by keeping away other thoughts. Such keeping away of other thoughts is now called meditation. But when the practice becomes firm, the real nature shows itself as true meditation.

D. Other thoughts arise more forcibly when one attempts meditation!

M. Yes, all kinds of thought arise in meditation. That is only right; for what lies hidden in you is brought out. Unless it rises up, how can it be destroyed? Thoughts rise up spontaneously, as it were, but only to be extinguished in due course, thus strengthening the mind.

D. There are times when persons and things take a vague, almost transparent form, as in a dream. One ceases to observe them as outside, but is passively conscious of their existence, while not actively conscious of any kind of selfhood. There is a deep quietness in the mind. Is it at such times that one is ready to dive into the Self? Or is this condition unhealthy, the result of self-hypnotism? Should it be encouraged as yielding temporary peace?

M. There is Consciousness along with quietness in the mind; this is exactly the state to be aimed at. The fact that the question has been framed on this point, without realizing that it is the Self, shows that the state is not steady but casual.

The word *diving* is appropriate when there are outgoing tendencies, and when, therefore, the mind has to be directed and turned within, there is a dip below the surface of externalities. But when quietness prevails without obstructing the Consciousness, where is the need to dive? If that state has not been realized as the Self, the effort to do so may be called diving. In this sense the state may be said to be suitable for realization or diving. Thus, the last two questions you have put do not arise.

D. The mind continues to feel partial toward children, possibly because the form of a child is often used to personify the Ideal. How can this preference be outgrown?

M. Hold on to the Self. Why think of children and of your reactions toward them?

D. This third visit to Tiruvannamalai seems to have intensified the sense of egoism in me and made meditation less easy. Is this an unimportant passing phase or a sign that I should avoid such places hereafter?

M. It is imaginary. This place or another is within you. Such imaginations must end; for places as such have nothing to do with the activities of the mind. Also your surroundings are not merely a matter of your individual choice; they are there as a matter of course; and you should rise above them and not get yourself entangled in them.

(A boy of eight and a half years sat in the hall at about five in the evening, when Śrī Bhagavan went up the hill. During His absence, the boy spoke on yoga and Vedānta in pure, simple, and literary Tamil, quoting freely from the sayings of saints and the sacred scriptures. When Śrī Bhagavan entered the hall, after nearly three-quarters of an hour, only silence prevailed. For the twenty minutes the boy sat in Śrī Bhagavan's presence, he spoke not a word but was merely gazing at Him. Then tears flowed from his eyes. He wiped them with his left hand and soon after left the place saying that he still awaits Self-realization.)

D. How should we explain the extraordinary characteristics of the boy?

M. The characteristics of his last birth are strong in him.

But however strong they may be, they do not manifest themselves save in a calm, still mind. It is within the experience of all that attempts to revive memory sometimes fail, while something flashes into the mind when it is calm and quiet.

D. How can the rebellious mind be made calm and tranquil?

M. Either see its source so that it may disappear, or surrender yourself so that it may be struck down. Self-surrender is the same as Self-knowledge, and either of them necessarily implies self-control. The ego submits only when it recognizes the Higher Power.

D. How can I escape from *saṃsāra,* which seems to be the real cause for making the mind restless? Is not renunciation an effective means to realize tranquillity of mind?

M. *Saṃsāra* is only in your mind. The world does not speak out saying, "Here I am, the world." If it did so, it would be ever there, making its presence felt by you even in your sleep. Since, however, it is not there in sleep, it is impermanent. Being impermanent, it lacks substance. Having no reality apart from the Self, it is easily subdued by the Self. The Self alone is permanent. Renunciation is the nonidentification of the Self with the not-Self. When the ignorance which identifies the Self with not-Self is removed, not-Self ceases to exist, and that is true renunciation.

D. Can we not perform actions without attachment even in the absence of such renunciation?

M. An *atma-jñāni* alone can be a good *karma-yogi.*

D. Does Bhagavan condemn Dvaita philosophy?

M. Dvaita can subsist only when you identify the Self with the not-Self. Advaita is nonidentification.

Bhakti and Jñāna

D. *Śrī Bhagavata* outlines a way to find Krishna in the Heart by prostrating to all and looking on all as the Lord Himself. Is this the right path leading to Self-realization? Is it not easier thus to adore Bhagavan in whatever meets the "mind" than to seek the Supramental through the mental inquiry "Who am I?"?

M. Yes, when you see God in all, do you think of God or do you not? You must certainly think of God for seeing God all around you. Keeping God in your mind becomes *dhyāna*, and *dhyāna* is the stage before Realization. Realization can only be in and of the Self. It can never be apart from the Self, and *dhyāna* must precede it. Whether you make *dhyāna* on God or on the Self, it is immaterial; for the goal is the same. You cannot by any means escape the Self. You want to see God in all, but not in yourself? If *all* is God, are you not included in that *all*? Being God yourself, is it a wonder that *all* is God? This is the method advised in *Śrī Bhagavata* and elsewhere by others. But even for this practice there must be the seer or thinker. Who is he?

D. How to see God, Who is all-pervasive?

M. To see God is to *be* God. There is no "all" apart from God for Him to pervade. He alone *is*.

D. Should we read the *Gītā* now and then?

M. Always.

D. What is the relation between *jñāna* and *bhakti*?

M. The eternal, unbroken, natural state of abiding in the Self is *jñāna*. To abide in the Self you must love the Self.

Since God is verily the Self, love of the Self is love of God; and that is *Bhakti*. *Jñāna* and *bhakti* are thus one and the same.

D. While making *nāma-japa* for an hour or more I fall into a state like sleep. On waking up I recollect that my *japa* has been interrupted, so I try again.

M. "Like sleep," that is right. It is the natural state. Because you are now associated with the ego, you consider that the natural state is something which interrupts your work. So you must have the experience repeated until you realize that it is your natural state. You will then find that *japa* is extraneous, but still it will go on automatically. Your present doubt is due to that false identity, namely of identifying yourself with the mind that does the *japa*. *Japa* means clinging to one thought to the exclusion of all other thoughts. That is its purpose. It leads to *dhyāna*, which ends in Self-realization or *jñāna*.

D. How should I carry on *nāma-japa*?

M. One should not use the Name of God mechanically and superficially without the feeling of devotion. To use the Name of God one must call upon Him with yearning and unreservedly surrender oneself to Him. Only after such surrender is the Name of God constantly with the man.

D. Where, then, is the need for inquiry or *vichāra*?

M. Surrender can take effect only when it is done with full knowledge as to what real surrender means. Such knowledge comes after inquiry and reflection and ends invariably in self-surrender. There is no difference between *jñāna* and absolute surrender to the Lord, that is, in thought, word, and deed. To be complete, surrender must be unquestioning; the devotee cannot bargain with the Lord or demand favors at His hands. Such entire surrender comprises all: it is *jñāna* and *vairāgya*, Devotion and Love.

Self and Individuality

D. Does not death dissolve the individuality of a person, so that there can be no rebirth, just as the rivers discharged into the ocean lose their individualities?

M. But when the waters evaporate and return as rain on the hills, they once more flow in the form of rivers and fall into the ocean; so also the individualities during sleep lose their separateness and yet return as individuals according to their *saṃskāras* or past tendencies. Even so it is in death; and the individuality of the person with *saṃskāras* is not lost.

D. How can that be?

M. See how a tree whose branches have been cut grows again. So long as the roots of the tree remain unimpaired, the tree will continue to grow. Similarly, the *saṃskāras*, which have merely sunk into the Heart on death, but have not perished for that reason, occasion rebirth at the right time; and that is how *jīvas* are reborn.

D. How could the innumerable *jīvas* and the wide universe whose existence is correlative to that of the *jīvas*, sprout up from such subtle *saṃskāras* sunk in the Heart?

M. Just as the big banyan tree sprouts from a tiny seed, so do the *jivas* and the whole universe with name and form sprout up from the subtle *saṃskāras*.

D. How does individuality emanate from the Absolute Self, and how is its return made possible?

M. As a spark proceeds from fire, individuality emanates from the Absolute Self. The spark is called the ego. In the case of the *ajñāni,* the ego identifies itself with some object simultaneously with its rise. It cannot remain without such association with objects.

This association is due to *ajñāna,* whose destruction is the objective of one's efforts. If this tendency to identify itself with objects is destroyed, the ego becomes pure and then it also merges into its Source. The false identification of oneself with the body is *dehātma-buddhi* or I-am-the-body idea. This must go before good results can follow.

D. How am I to eradicate it?

M. You exist in *suṣupti* without being associated with the body and the mind, but in the other two states you are associated with them. If you were one with the body, how could you exist without the body in *suṣupti*? You can separate yourself from what is external to you but not from that which is one with you. Hence the ego cannot be one with the body. This must be realized in the waking state. The three states are studied in order to gain this knowledge.

D. How can the ego, which is confined to two of the states, endeavor to realize That which comprises all the three states?

M. The ego in its purity is experienced in the intervals between two states or between two thoughts. The ego is like the worm which leaves one hold only after it catches another. Its true nature is known when it is out of contact with objects or thoughts. You should realize this interval as the abiding, unchangeable Reality, your true Being, through the conviction gained by the study of the three states, *jāgrat, svapna,* and *suṣupti.*

D. Can I not remain in *suṣupti* as long as I like and also be in it at will, just as I am in the waking state? What is the *jñāni*'s experience of these three states?

M. *Suṣupti* does exist in your waking state also. You are in *suṣupti* even now. That should be consciously entered into and reached in this very waking state. There is no real going in and coming out of it. To be aware of *suṣupti* in the *jāgrat* state is *jāgrat-suṣupti* and that is *samādhi.*

The *ajñāni* cannot remain long in *suṣupti,* because he is forced by his nature to emerge from it. His ego is not dead and it will rise again and again. But the *jñāni* crushes the ego at its Source. It may seem to emerge at times in his case also as if impelled by *prārabdha.* That is, in the case of the *jñāni* also, for all outward purposes *prārabdha* would seem to sustain or keep up the ego, as in the case of the *ajñāni;* but there is this fundamental difference, that the *ajñāni*'s ego when it rises up (really it has never subsided except in deep sleep) is quite ignorant of its Source: in other words, the *ajñāni* is not aware of his *suṣupti* in his dream and waking states: in the case of the *jñāni,* on the contrary, the rise or existence of the ego is only apparent, and he enjoys his unbroken, transcendental Experience in spite of such apparent rise or existence of the ego, keeping his attention (*lakṣya*) always on the Source. This ego is harmless; it is merely like the skeleton of a burnt rope—though with a form, it is useless to tie up anything. By constantly keeping one's attention on the Source, the ego is dissolved in that Source like a salt-doll in the sea.

D. What is the significance of the Crucifixion?

M. The body is the cross. Jesus, the son of man, is the ego or I-am-the-body idea. When the son of man is crucified on the cross, the ego perishes, and what survives is the Absolute Being. It is the resurrection of the Glorious Self, of the Christ—the Son of God.

D. But how is crucifixion justified? Is not killing a terrible crime?

M. Everyone is committing suicide. The eternal, blissful, natural State has been smothered by this ignorant life. In this way the present life is due to the killing of the eternal, positive Existence. Is it not really a case of suicide? So why worry about killing?

D. Śrī Ramakrishna says that *nirvikalpa samādhi* cannot last longer than twenty-one days; if persisted in, the person dies. Is this a fact?

M. When the *prārabdha* is exhausted, the ego is completely dissolved, without leaving any trace behind. This is the final Liberation (*nirvāṇa*). Unless *prārabdha* is exhausted, the ego will rise up, as it may appear to do in the case of *jīvanmuktas*.

Self-Realization

D. How can I attain Self-realization?

M. Realization is nothing to be gained afresh; it is already there. All that is necessary is to get rid of the thought "I have not realized."

Stillness or Peace is Realization. There is no moment when the Self is not. So long as there is doubt or the feeling of non-Realization, the attempt should be made to rid oneself of these thoughts. They are due to the identification of the Self with the not-Self. When the not-Self disappears, the Self alone remains. To make room, it is enough that the cramping be removed; room is not brought in from elsewhere.

D. Since Realization is not possible without *vāsanā-kṣaya,* how am I to realize that state in which the *vāsanās* are effectively destroyed?

M. You are in that state now!

D. Does it mean that by holding on to the Self, the *vāsanās* should be destroyed as and when they emerge?

M. They will themselves be destroyed if you remain as you are.

D. How shall I reach the Self?

M. There is no reaching the Self. If the Self were to be reached, it would mean that the Self is not here and now but is yet to be obtained. What is got afresh will also be lost. So it will be impermanent. What is not permanent is not worth striving for. So I say the Self is not reached. You *are* the Self; you are already That.

The fact is, you are ignorant of your blissful state. Ignorance supervenes and draws a veil over the pure Self, which is Bliss. Attempts are directed only to remove this veil of ignorance, which is merely wrong knowledge. The wrong knowledge is the false identification of the self with the body, mind, etc. This false identification must go, and then the Self alone remains.

Therefore Realization is for everyone; Realization makes no differences between aspirants. This very doubt whether you can realize and the notion "I have not realized" are themselves the obstacles. Be free from these obstacles also.

D. What is the use of *samādhi,* and does thought subsist then?

M. *Samādhi* alone can reveal the Truth. Thoughts cast a veil over Reality, and so It is not realized as such in states other than *samādhi.* In *samādhi* there is only the feeling "I am" and no thoughts. The experience "I am" is *being still.*

D. How can I repeat the experience of *samādhi* or the stillness that I obtain here?

M. Your present experience is due to the influence of the atmosphere in which you find yourself. Can you have it outside this atmosphere? The experience is spasmodic. Until it becomes permanent, practice is necessary.

D. One has at times vivid flashes of a consciousness whose center is outside the normal self and which seems to be all-inclusive. Without concerning ourselves with philosophical concepts, how would Bhagavan advise me to work toward getting, retaining, and extending those rare flashes? Does *abhyāsa* in such experience involve retirement?

M. Outside! For whom is the inside or outside? These can exist only so long as there are subject and object. For whom are these two again? On investigation you will find that they resolve into the subject only. See who is the subject; and this inquiry leads you to pure Consciousness beyond the subject.

The *normal self* is the mind. This mind is with limitations. But pure Consciousness is beyond limitations and is reached by investigation as above outlined.

Getting: The Self is always there. You have only to remove the veil obstructing the revelation of the Self.

Retaining: Once you realize the Self, it becomes your direct and immediate experience. It is never lost.

Extending: There is no extending of the Self, for it is as ever, without contraction or expansion.

Retirement: Abiding in the Self is solitude. Because there is nothing alien to the Self. Retirement must be from some one place or state to another. There is neither the one nor the other apart from the Self. *All* being the Self, retirement is impossible and inconceivable.

Abhyāsa is only the prevention of disturbance to the inherent peace. You are always in your natural state whether you make *abhyāsa* or not. . . . To remain as you are, without question or doubt, is your natural state.

D. On realizing *samādhi,* does one not obtain *siddhis* also?

M. In order to display *siddhis,* there must be others to recognize them. That means there is no *jñāna* in the one who displays them. Therefore, *siddhis* are not worth a thought: *jñāna* alone is to be aimed at and gained.

D. Does my Realization help others?

M. Yes, and it is the best help that you can possibly render to others. Those who have discovered great truths have done so in the still depths of the Self. But really there are no "others" to be helped. For the Realized Being sees only the Self, just as the goldsmith sees only the gold while valuing it in various jewels made of gold. When you identify yourself with the body, name and form are there. But when you transcend the body-consciousness, the "others" also disappear. The Realized One does not see the world as different from himself.

D. Would it not be better if the saints mix with others?

M. There are no "others" to mix with. The Self is the only Reality.

D. Should I not try to help the suffering world?

M. The Power that created you has created the world as well. If It can take care of you, It can similarly take care of the world also. . . . If God has created the world, it is His business to look after it, not yours.

D. Is it not our duty to be patriots?

M. Your duty is *to be,* and not to be this or that. "I am that I am" sums up the whole truth: the method is summarized in "be still."

And what does Stillness mean? It means "Destroy yourself"; because every name and form is the cause of trouble. "I-I" is the Self. "I am this" is the ego. When the "I" is kept up as the "I" only, it is the Self. When it flies off at a tangent and says "I am this or that, I am such and such,"—it is the ego.

D. Who then is God?

M. The Self is God. "I am" is God. If God is apart from the Self, He must be a selfless God, which is absurd.

All that is required to realize the Self is to *be still.* What can be easier than that? Hence *ātma-vidya* is the easiest to attain.

Guru and His Grace

D. What is *Guru-kṛpa*? How does it lead to Self-realization?

M. *Guru* is the Self. . . . Sometimes a man becomes dissatisfied with his life, and, not content with what he has, he seeks the satisfaction of his desires, through prayer to God, etc. His mind is gradually purified until he longs to know God, more to obtain His grace than to satisfy his worldly desires. Then, God's grace begins to manifest. God takes the form of a Guru and appears to the devotee, teaches him the Truth, and, moreover, purifies his mind by association. The devotee's mind gains strength and is then able to turn inward. By meditation it is further purified and it remains still without the least ripple. That calm expanse is the Self.

The Guru is both "external" and "internal." From the "exterior" he gives a push to the mind to turn inward; from the "interior" he pulls the mind toward the Self and helps in the quieting of the mind. That is *guru-kṛpa*. There is no difference between God, Guru, and the Self.

D. In the Theosophical Society they meditate in order to seek Masters to guide them.

M. The Master is within; meditation is meant to remove the ignorant idea that he is only outside. If he is a stranger whom you await, he is bound to disappear also. Where is the use for a transient being like that? But as long as you think you are separate or that you are the body, so long is the Master "without" also necessary, and he will appear as if with a body. When the wrong identification of oneself with the body ceases, the Master will be found as none other than the Self.

D. Will the Guru help us to know the Self through initiation and so forth?

M. Does the Guru hold you by the hand and whisper in your ear? You may imagine him to be what you are yourself. Because you think you are with a body, you think he has also a body, to do something tangible to you. His work lies within, in the spiritual realm.

D. How is the Guru found?

M. God, Who is immanent, in His grace takes pity on the loving devotee and manifests Himself according to the devotee's development. The devotee thinks that He is a man and expects a relationship as between two physical bodies. But the Guru, who is God or the Self incarnate, works from within, helps the man to see the error of his ways, and guides him in the right path until he realizes the Self within.

D. What should the devotee do, then?

M. He has only to live up to the words of the Master and work within. The Master is both "within" and "without," so he creates conditions to drive you inward and at the same time prepares the "interior" to drag you to the Center. Thus he gives a push from "without" and exerts a pull from "within," so that you may be fixed at the Center.

You think that the world can be conquered by your own efforts. When you are frustrated externally and are driven inward, you feel, "Oh! there is a Power Higher than man!"

The ego is like a very powerful elephant which cannot be brought under control by any less powerful than a lion, which, in this instance, is no other than the Guru, whose very look makes the elephantlike ego tremble and die.

You will know in due course that your glory lies where you cease to exist. In order to gain that state, you should surrender yourself. Then the Master sees that you are in a fit state to receive guidance, and he guides you.

D. How can the Silence of the Guru, who gives no initiation nor does any other tangible act, be more powerful than his word? How is such Silence better than the study of scriptures?

M. Silence is the most potent form of work. However vast and emphatic the scriptures may be, they fail in their effect. The Guru is quiet, and grace prevails in all. This Silence is more vast and more emphatic than all the scriptures put together.

D. But can the devotee obtain happiness?

M. The devotee surrenders himself to the Master, and it means that there is no vestige of individuality retained by him. If the surrender is complete, all sense of self is lost, and then there can be no misery or sorrow. The Eternal Being is nothing but Happiness. That comes as a revelation.

D. How can I obtain grace?

M. Grace is the Self. That also is not to be acquired: you only need to know that it exists.

The sun is brightness only. It does not see darkness. Yet you speak of darkness fleeing on the sun's approach. So also the devotee's ignorance, like the phantom of darkness, vanishes at the look of the Guru. You are surrounded by sunlight; yet if you would see the sun, you must turn in its direction and look at it. So also grace is found by the proper approach you make, though it is here and now.

D. Cannot grace hasten ripeness in the seeker?

M. Leave it all to the Master. Surrender to him without reserve.

One of two things must be done: either surrender yourself, because you realize your inability and need a Higher Power to help you; or investigate the cause of misery, go into the Source, and so merge in the Self. Either way, you will be free from misery. God or Guru never forsakes the devotee who has surrendered himself.

D. What is the significance of prostration to the Guru or God?

M. Prostration signifies the subsidence of the ego, and it means merging into the Source. God or Guru cannot be deceived by outward genuflections, bowing, and prostrations. He sees whether the ego is there or not.

D. Will not Bhagavan give me some *prasād* from his leaf as a mark of his grace?

M. Eat without thinking of the ego. Then what you eat becomes Bhagavan's *prasād.*

D. Is not the literate man better qualified for Enlightenment in the sense that he stands in no need of *Guru-kṛpa*?

M. Even a learned man must bow before the illiterate sage. Illiteracy is ignorance and education is learned ignorance. Both are ignorant of the true aim. The Sage is ignorant in a different line. He is ignorant because there is no "other" for him.

D. Is it not to obtain the guru's grace that presents are offered to him? So the visitors offer presents to Bhagavan.

M. Why do they bring presents? Do I want them? Even if I refuse, they thrust the presents on me! What for? Is it not like giving a bait to catch the fish? Is the angler anxious to feed them? No, he is anxious to feed on the fish!

D. Is the Theosophical idea of giving successive initiations before attaining *mokṣa* true?

M. Those who attain *mokṣa* in one life must have passed through all the initiations in their former lives.

D. Theosophy says that *jñānis* after death have to choose four or five lines of work, not necessarily in this world. What is Bhagavan's opinion?

M. Some may take up work, but not all.

D. Are you conscious of a brotherhood of invisible *ṛṣis*?

M. If invisible, how can you see them?

D. In consciousness.

M. There is nothing external in Consciousness.

D. Can I realize them?

M. If you realize your own Reality, then that of the *ṛṣis* and Masters will become clear to you. There is only one Master, and that is the Self.

D. Is reincarnation true?

M. Reincarnation exists only so long as there is ignorance. There is really no reincarnation at all, either now or before. Nor will there be any hereafter. This is the truth.

D. Can a yogi know his past lives?

M. Do you know the present life that you wish to know the past? Find the present, then the rest will follow. Even with your present limited knowledge, you suffer so much; why should you burden yourself with more knowledge? Is it to suffer more?

D. Does Bhagavan use occult powers to make others realize the Self, or is the mere fact of Bhagavan's Realization enough for that?

M. The spiritual force of Self-realization is far more powerful than the use of all the occult powers. Inasmuch as there is no ego in the Sage, there are no "others" for him. What is the highest benefit that can be conferred on you? It is happiness, and happiness is born of peace. Peace can reign only where there is no disturbance, and disturbance is due to thoughts that arise in the mind. When the mind itself is absent, there will be perfect peace. Unless a person has annihilated the mind, he cannot gain peace and be happy. And unless he himself is happy, he cannot bestow happiness on "others." Since, however, there are no "others" for the Sage who has no mind, the mere fact of his Self-realization is itself enough to make the "others" happy.

Peace and Happiness

D. How can I get peace? I do not seem to obtain it through *vichāra.*

M. Peace is your natural state. It is the mind that obstructs the natural state. Your *vichāra* has been made only in the mind. Investigate what the mind is, and it will disappear. There is no such thing as mind apart from thought. Nevertheless, because of the emergence of thought, you surmise something from which it starts and term that the mind. When you probe to see what it is, you find there is really no such thing as mind. When the mind has thus vanished, you realize eternal Peace.

D. Through poetry, music, *japa, bhajana,* the sight of beautiful landscapes, reading the lines of spiritual verses, etc., one experiences sometimes a true sense of all unity. Is that feeling of deep blissful quiet (wherein the personal self has no place) the same as the entering into the Heart of which Bhagavan speaks? Will practice thereof lead to a deeper *samādhi* and so ultimately to a full vision of the Real?

M. There is happiness when agreeable things are presented to the mind. It is the happiness inherent to the Self, and there is no other happiness. And it is not alien and afar. You are diving into the Self on those occasions which you consider pleasurable; that diving results in self-existent bliss. But the association of ideas is responsible for foisting that bliss on other things or occurrences while, in fact, that bliss is within you. On these occasions you are plunging into the Self, though unconsciously. If you do so consciously, with the conviction that comes of the experience that you are identical with the happiness which is verily the Self, the one Reality, you call it Realization. I want you to dive consciously into the Self, i.e., into the Heart.

Self-Inquiry

D. How is one to realize the Self?

M. Whose Self? Find out.

D. Mine, but who am I?

M. Find out yourself.

D. I don't know how.

M. Just think over the question. Who is it that says, "I don't know"? Who is the "I" in your statement? What is not known?

D. Somebody or something in me.

M. Who is that somebody? In whom?

D. Perhaps some power.

M. Find out.

D. Why was I born?

M. Who was born? The answer is the same to all your questions.

D. Who am I, then?

M. (Smiling) You have come to examine me? *You* must say who you are.

D. However much I may try, I do not seem to catch the "I." It is not even clearly discernible.

M. Who is it that says that the "I" is not discernible? Are there two "I's" in you that one is not discernible by the other?

D. Instead of inquiring "Who am I?," can I put the question to myself "Who are *You?*," since then my mind may be fixed on You whom I consider to be God in the form of Guru. Perhaps, I would be nearer the goal of my quest by that inquiry than by asking myself "Who am I?"

M. Whatever form your inquiry may take, you must finally come to the one "I," the Self. All these distinctions made between the "I" and "you," Master and disciple, etc., are merely a sign of one's ignorance. The "I" Supreme alone is. To think otherwise is to delude oneself.

A story from the Puranas about Sage Ribhu and his disciple Nidagha is particularly instructive in this context.

Although Ribhu taught his disciple the supreme Truth of the One Brahman without a second, Nidagha, in spite of his erudition and understanding, did not get sufficient conviction to adopt and follow the path of *jñāna,* but settled down in his native town to lead a life devoted to the observance of ceremonial religion.

But the Sage loved his disciple as deeply as the latter venerated his Master. In spite of his age, Ribhu would himself go to his disciple in the town, just to see how far the latter had outgrown his ritualism. At times the Sage went in disguise, so that he might observe how Nidagha would act when he did not know that he was being observed by his Master.

On one such occasion Ribhu, who had put on the disguise of a village rustic, found Nidagha intently watching a royal procession. Unrecognized by the town-dweller Nidagha, the village rustic inquired what the bustle was all about, and was told that the king was going in procession.

"Oh! It is the king. He goes in procession! But where is he?" asked the rustic.

"There, on the elephant," said Nidagha.

"You say the king is on the elephant. Yes, I see the two," said the rustic. "But which is the king and which is the elephant?"

"What!" exclaimed Nidagha. "You see the two, but do not know that the man above is the king and the animal below is the elephant? What is the use of talking to a man like you?"

"Pray, be not impatient with an ignorant man like me," begged the rustic. "But you said 'above' and 'below'—what do they mean?

Nidagha could stand it no more. "You see the king and the elephant, the one *above* and the other *below.* Yet you want to know what is meant by 'above' and 'below'?" burst out Nidagha. "If things seen and words spoken can convey so little to you, action alone can teach you. Bend forward, and you will know it all too well."

The rustic did as he was told. Nidagha got on his shoulders and said, "Know it now. I am *above* as the king, you are *below* as the elephant. Is that clear enough?"

"No, not yet," was the rustic's quiet reply. "You say you are above like the king and I am below like the elephant. The 'king,' the 'elephant,' 'above,' and 'below,' so far it is clear. But pray, tell me what you mean by '*I*' and '*you*'?"

When Nidagha was thus confronted all of a sudden with the mighty problem of defining the "you" apart from the "I," light dawned on his mind. At once he jumped down and fell at his Master's feet, saying, "Who else but my venerable Master, Ribhu, could have thus drawn my mind from the superficialities of physical existence to the true Being of Self? O benign Master, I crave thy blessings."

Therefore, while your aim is to transcend here and now these superficialities of physical existence through *ātma-vichāra,* where is the scope for making the distinctions of "you" and "I," which pertain only to the body? When you turn the mind within, seeking the Source of thought, where is the "you" and where is the "I"?

You should seek and be the Self that includes all.

D. But is it not funny that the "I" should be searching for the "I"? Does not the inquiry "Who am I?" turn out in the end an empty formula? Or am I to put the question to myself endlessly, repeating it like some *mantra?*

M. Self-inquiry is certainly not an empty formula; it is more than the repetition of any *mantra.* If the inquiry "Who am I?" were a mere mental questioning, it would not be of much value. The very purpose of Self-inquiry is to focus the entire mind at its Source. It is not, therefore, a case of one "I" searching for another "I."

Much less is Self-inquiry an empty formula, for it involves an intense activity of the entire mind to keep it steadily poised in pure Self-awareness.

Self-inquiry is the one infallible means, the only direct one, to realize the unconditioned, absolute Being that you really are.

D. Why should Self-inquiry alone be considered the direct means to *jñāna?*

M. Because every kind of *sadhana* except that of *ātma-vichāra* presupposes the retention of the mind as the instrument for carrying on the *sādhana,* and without the mind it cannot be practiced. The ego may take different and subtler forms at the different stages of one's practice, but is itself never destroyed.

When Janaka exclaimed, "Now I have discovered the thief who has been ruining me all along. He shall be dealt with summarily," the king was really referring to the ego or the mind.

D. But the thief may well be apprehended by the other *sādhanas* as well.

M. The attempt to destroy the ego or the mind through *sādhanas* other than *ātma-vichāra* is just like the thief turning out a policeman to catch the thief, that is, himself. *Ātma-vichāra* alone can reveal the truth that neither the ego nor the mind really exists, and enables one to realize the pure, undifferentiated Being of the Self or the Absolute.

Having realized the Self, nothing remains to be known, because it is perfect Bliss; it is the All.

D. In this life beset with limitations, can I ever realize the Bliss of the Self?

M. That Bliss of the Self is always with you, and you will find it for yourself, if you seek it earnestly.

The cause of your misery is not in the life without; it is in you as the ego. You impose limitations on yourself and then make a vain struggle to transcend them. All unhappiness is due to the ego; with it comes all your trouble. What does it avail you to attribute to the happenings in life the cause of misery which is really within you? What happiness can you get from things extraneous to yourself? When you get it, how long will it last?

If you would deny the ego and scorch it by ignoring it, you would be free. If you accept it, it will impose limitations on you and throw you into a vain struggle to transcend them. That was how the thief sought to "ruin" King Janaka.

To *be* the Self that you really are is the only means to realize the Bliss that is ever yours.

D. Not having realized the Truth that the Self alone exists, should I not adopt *bhakti* and *yoga-margas* as being more suitable for purposes of *sādhana* than *vichāra marga*? Is not the realization of one's absolute Being that is, *Brahma-jñāna,* something quite unattainable to a layman like me?

M. *Brahma-jñāna* is not a knowledge to be acquired, so that acquiring it one may obtain happiness. It is one's ignorant outlook that one should give up. The Self you seek to know is verily yourself. Your supposed ignorance causes you needless grief, like that of the ten foolish men who grieved the "loss" of the tenth man who was never lost.

The ten foolish men in the parable forded a stream and on reaching the other shore wanted to make sure that all of them had in fact safely crossed the stream. One of the ten began to count, but while counting others left himself out. "I see only nine; sure enough, we have lost one. Who can it be?" he said. "Did you count correctly?" asked another, and did the counting himself. But he too counted only nine. One after the other, each of the ten counted only nine, missing himself. "We are only nine," they all agreed, "but who is the missing one?" they asked themselves. Every effort they made to discover the "missing" individual failed. "Whoever he be that is drowned," said the most sentimental of ten fools, "we have lost him." So saying, he burst into tears, and the rest of the nine followed suit.

Seeing them, weeping on the river bank, a sympathetic wayfarer inquired for the cause. They related what had happened and said that even after counting themselves several times they could find no more than nine. On hearing the story, but seeing all the ten before him, the wayfarer guessed what had happened. In order to make them know for themselves that they were really ten, that all of them had come safe from the crossing, he told them, "Let each of you count for himself but one after the other serially, one, two, three and so on, while I shall give you each a blow so that all of you may be sure of having been included in the count, and included only once. The tenth 'missing' man will then be found." Hearing this, they rejoiced at the prospect of finding their "lost" comrade and accepted the method suggested by the wayfarer.

While the kind wayfarer gave a blow to each of the ten in turn, he that got the blow counted himself aloud. "Ten," said the last man as he got the last blow in his turn. Bewildered, they looked at one another. "We *are* ten," they said with one voice and thanked the wayfarer for having removed their grief.

That is the parable. From where was the tenth man brought in? Was he ever lost? By knowing that he had been there all the while, did they learn anything new? The cause of their grief was not the real loss of any one of the ten; it was their own ignorance, rather their mere supposition that one of them was lost (though they could not find who he was) because they counted only nine.

Such is also the case with you. Truly there is no cause for you to be miserable and unhappy. You yourself impose limitations on your true nature of infinite Being and then weep that you are but a finite creature. Then you take up this or that *sādhana* to transcend the nonexistent limitations. But if your *sādhana* itself assumes the existence of the limitations, how can it help you to transcend them?

Hence I say know that you are really the infinite, pure Being, the Self Absolute. You are always that Self and nothing but that Self. Therefore, you can never be really ignorant of the Self; your ignorance is merely a formal ignorance, like the ignorance of the ten fools about the "lost" tenth man. It is this ignorance that caused them grief.

Know then that true Knowledge does not create a new Being for you; it only removes your "ignorant ignorance." Bliss is not added to your nature; it is merely revealed as your true and natural state, eternal and imperishable. The only way to be rid of your grief is to *know* and *be* the Self. How can this be unattainable?

Sādhana and Grace

D. Research on God has been going on from time immemorial. Has the final word been said?

M. (Keeps silence for some time)

D. (Puzzled) Should I consider Śrī Bhagavan's silence as the reply to my question?

M. Yes. *Mouna* is *Īsvara-svarūpa*. Hence the text: "The Truth of Supreme *Brahman* proclaimed through Silent Eloquence."

D. Buddha is said to have ignored such inquiries about God.

M. And for this he was called a *śūnyavādin* (nihilist). In fact Buddha concerned himself more with directing the seeker to realize Bliss here and now than with academic discussion about God, etc.

D. God is described as manifest and unmanifest. As the former He is said to include the world as a part of His Being. If that is so, we as part of that world should have easily known Him in the manifested form.

M. Know yourself before you seek to decide about the nature of God and the world.

D. Does knowing myself imply knowing God?

M. Yes, God is within you.

D. Then what stands in the way of my knowing myself or God?

M. Your wandering mind and perverted ways.

D. I am a weak creature. But why does not the superior power of the Lord within remove the obstacles?

M. Yes, He will, if you have the aspiration.

D. Why should He not create the aspiration in me?

M. Then surrender yourself.

D. If I surrender myself, is no prayer to God necessary?

M. Surrender itself is a mighty prayer.

D. But is it not necessary to understand His nature before one surrenders oneself?

M. If you believe that God will do for you all the things you want Him to do, then surrender yourself to Him. Otherwise let God alone, and know yourself.

D. Has God or the Guru any solicitude for me?

M. If you seek either—they are not really two but one and identical—rest assured that they are seeking you with a solicitude greater than you can ever imagine.

D. Jesus gave the parable of the lost coin, wherein the woman searches for it till it is found.

M. Yes, that aptly represents the truth that God or the Guru is always in search of the earnest seeker. Were the coin a dud piece, the woman would not have made that long search. Do you see what it means? The seeker must qualify himself through devotion, etc.

D. But one may not be quite sure of God's grace.

M. If the unripe mind does not feel His grace, it does not mean that God's grace is absent, for it would imply that God is at times not gracious, that is, ceases to be God.

D. Is that the same as the saying of Christ, "According to thy faith be it done unto thee"?

M. Quite so.

D. The Upanishads say, I am told, that he alone knows the *Ātman* whom the *Ātman* chooses. Why should the *Ātman* choose at all? If it chooses, why some particular person?

M. When the sun rises, some buds alone blossom, not all. Do you blame the sun for that? Nor can the bud blossom of itself; it requires the sunlight to do it.

D. May we not say that the help of the *Ātman* is needed because it is the *Ātman* that drew over itself the veil of *māyā?*

M. You may say so.

D. If the *Ātman* has drawn the veil over itself, should not itself remove the veil?

M. It will do so. See for whom is the veil.

D. Why should I? Let the *Ātman* itself remove the veil!

M. If the *Ātman* talks about the veil, then the *Ātman* itself will remove it.

D. Is God personal?

M. Yes, He is always the first person, the "I," ever standing before you. Because you give precedence to worldly things, God appears to have receded to the background. If you give up all else and seek Him alone, He alone will remain as the "I," the Self.

D. The final state of Realization is said to be according to Advaita the absolute union with the Divine and according to Viśiṣṭādvaita a qualified union, while Dvaita maintains that there is no union at all. Which of these should be considered the correct view?

M. Why speculate as to what will happen some time in the future? All are agreed that the "I" exists. To whichever school of thought he may belong, let the earnest seeker first find out what the "I" is. Then it will be time enough to know what the final state will be, whether the "I" will get merged in the Supreme Being or stand apart from Him. Let us not forestall the conclusion, but keep an open mind.

D. But will not some understanding of the final state be a helpful guide even to the aspirant?

M. No purpose is served in trying to decide now what the final state of Realization will be. It has no intrinsic value.

D. Why so?

M. Because you proceed on a wrong principle. Your ascertainment has to depend on the intellect, which shines only by the light it derives from the Self. Is it not presumptuous on the part of the intellect to sit in judgment over that of which it is but a limited manifestation, and from which it derives its little light?

How can the intellect, which can never reach the Self, be competent to ascertain, much less decide, the nature of the final state of Realization? It is like trying to measure the sunlight at its source by the standard of the light given by a candle. The wax will melt down before the candle comes anywhere near the sun.

Instead of indulging in mere speculation, devote yourself here and now to the search for the Truth that is ever within you.

The Jñāni and the World

D. Is the world perceived by the *jñāni?*

M. From whom is the question? Is it from a *jñāni* or *ajñāni?*

D. From an *ajñāni,* I admit.

M. Is it the world that seeks to decide the issue about its reality? The doubt arises in you. Know in the first instance who the doubter is, and then you may consider if the world is real or not.

D. The *ajñāni* sees and knows the world and its objects, which affect his senses of touch, taste, etc. Does the *jñāni* experience the world in like manner?

M. You talk of seeing and knowing the world. But without knowing yourself, the knowing subject (without whom there is no knowledge of the object), how can you know the true nature of the world, the known object? No doubt, the objects affect the body and the sense organs, but is it to your body that the question arises? Does the body say, "I feel the object, it is real"? Or is it the world that says to you, "I, the world, am real"?

D. I am only trying to understand the *jñāni*'s point of view about the world. Is the world perceived after Self-realization?

M. Why worry yourself about the world and what happens to it after Self-realization? First realize the Self. What does it matter if the world is perceived or not? Do you gain anything to help you in your quest by the non-perception of the world during sleep? Conversely, what would you lose now by the perception of the world? It is quite immaterial to the *jñāni* or *ajñāni* if he perceives the world or not. It is seen by both, but their viewpoints differ.

D. If the *jñāni* and the *ajñāni* perceive the world in like manner, where is the difference between them?

M. Seeing the world, the *jñāni* sees the Self which is the substratum of all that is seen; the *ajñāni*, whether he sees the world or not, is ignorant of his true being, the Self.

Take the instance of moving pictures on the screen in the cinema show. What is there in front of you before the play begins? Merely the screen. On that screen you see the entire show, and for all appearances the pictures are real. But go and try to take hold of them. What do you take hold of? Merely the screen on which the pictures appeared so real. After the play, when the pictures disappear, what remains? The screen again!

So with the Self. That alone exists; the pictures come and go. If you hold on to the Self, you will not be deceived by the appearance of the pictures. Nor does it matter at all if the pictures appear or disappear. Ignoring the Self, the *ajñāni* thinks the world is real, just as, ignoring the screen, he sees merely the pictures, as if they existed apart from it. If one knows that without the Seer there is nothing to be seen, just as there are no pictures without the screen, one is not deluded. The *jñāni* knows that the screen, the pictures, and the sight thereof are but the Self. With the pictures the Self is in its manifest form; without the pictures It remains in the unmanifest form. To the *jñāni* it is quite immaterial if the Self is in the one form or the other. He is always the Self. But the *ajñāni*, seeing the *jñāni* active, gets confounded.

D. It is just that point that prompted me to put my first question, whether one who has realized the Self perceives the world as we do, and if he does, I should like to know how Śrī Bhagavan felt about the mysterious disappearance of the photo yesterday. . . .

M. (Smiling) You are referring to the photo of the Madura temple. A few minutes earlier it was passing through the hands of the visitors, who looked at it in turn. Evidently, it was mislaid among the pages of some book or other that they were consulting.

D. Yes, it was that incident. How does Bhagavan view it? There was an anxious search for the photo, which, in the end, could not be found. How does Bhagavan view the mysterious disappearance of the photo just at the moment when it was wanted?

M. Suppose you dream that you are taking me to your distant country, Poland. You wake up and ask me, "I dreamt so and so. Did you also have some such dream or know in some other way that I was taking you to Poland?" What significance will you attach to such an inquiry?

D. But, with regard to the missing photo, the whole incident took place in front of Śrī Bhagavan.

M. The seeing of the photo, its disappearance, as well as your present inquiry, are all mere workings of mind.

There is a story in the Puranas which illustrates the point. When Sita was missing from the forest hermitage, Rama went about in search of her, wailing, "O Sita, Sita!" It is said that Parvati and Parameshvara saw from above what was taking place in the forest. Parvati expressed her surprise to Shiva and said, "You praised Rama as the perfect being. See how he behaves and grieves at the loss of Sita!" Shiva replied, "If you are skeptical about Rama's perfection, then put him to the test yourself. Through your *yoga-māyā* transform yourself into the likeness of Sita and appear before him." Parvati did so. She appeared before Rama in the very likeness of Sita, but to her astonishment Rama ignored her presence and went on as before, calling out, "O Sita, O Sita!" as if he were blind.

D. I am unable to grasp the moral of the story.

M. If Rama were really searching for the bodily presence

of Sita, he would have recognized the person who was standing in front of him as the Sita he had lost. But no, the missing Sita was just as unreal as the Sita that appeared before his eyes. Rama was not really blind; but to Rama, the *jñāni,* the prior being of Sita in the hermitage, her disappearance, his consequent search for her as well as the actual presence of Parvati in the guise of Sita, were all equally unreal. Do you now understand how the missing photo was viewed?

D. I cannot say it is all clear to me. Is the world that is seen, felt, and sensed by us in so many ways something like a dream, an illusion?

M. There is no alternative for you but to accept the world as unreal, if you are seeking the Truth and the Truth alone.

D. Why so?

M. For the simple reason that unless you give up the idea that the world is real your mind will always be after it. If you take the appearance to be real you will never know the Real itself, although it is the Real alone that exists. This point is illustrated by the analogy of the snake and the rope. As long as you see the snake, you cannot see the rope as such. The nonexistent snake becomes real to you, while the real rope seems wholly nonexistent as such.

D. It is easy to accept tentatively that the world is not ultimately real, but it is hard to have the conviction that it is really unreal.

M. Even so is your dream world real while you are dreaming. So long as the dream lasts, everything you see and feel therein is real.

D. Is then the world nothing better than a dream?

M. What is wrong with the sense of reality you have while you are dreaming? You may be dreaming of something quite impossible, for instance, of having a happy chat with a dead person. Just for a moment you may doubt in the dream, saying to yourself, "Was he not dead?" But somehow your mind reconciles itself to the dream vision, and the person is as good as alive for the purposes of the dream. In other words, the dream as a dream does not permit you to doubt its reality. Even so, you are unable to doubt the reality of the world of your wakeful experience. How can the mind which has itself created the world accept it as unreal? That is the significance of the comparison made between the world of wakeful experience and the dream world. Both are but creations of the mind, and so long as the mind is engrossed in either, it finds itself unable to deny the reality of the dream world while dreaming and of the waking world while awake. If, on the contrary, you withdraw your mind completely from the world and turn it within and abide thus, that is, if you keep awake always to the Self, which is the substratum of all experience, you will find the world, of which alone you are now aware, just as unreal as the world in which you lived in your dream.

D. As I said before, we see, feel, and sense the world in so many ways. These sensations are the reactions to the objects seen, felt, etc., and are not mental creations as in dreams, which differ not only from person to person but also with regard to the same person. Is that not enough to prove the objective reality of the world?

M. All this talk about inconsistencies and their attribution to the dream world arises only now, when you are awake. While you were dreaming, the dream was a perfectly integrated whole. That is to say, if you felt thirsty in a dream, the illusory drinking of illusory water did quench your illusory thirst. But all this was real and not illusory to you so long as you did not know that the dream itself was illusory. Similarly with the waking world; and the sensations you now have get coordinated to give you the impression that the world is real.

If, on the contrary, the world is a self-existent reality (that is what you evidently mean by its objectivity), what prevents the world from revealing itself to you in sleep? You do not say you have not existed in your sleep.

D. Neither do I deny the world's existence while I am asleep. It has been existing all the while. If during my sleep I did not see it, others who are not sleeping saw it.

M. To say you existed while asleep, was it necessary to call in the evidence of others so as to prove it to you? Why do you seek their evidence now? Those "others" can tell you of having seen the world (during your sleep) only when you yourself are awake. With regard to your own existence it is different. On waking up you say you had a sound sleep, so that to that extent you are aware of yourself in the deepest sleep, whereas you have not the slightest notion of the world's existence then. Even now, while you are awake, is it the world that says, "I am real," or is it you?

D. Of course *I* say it, but I say it of the world.

M. Well, then, that world, which you say is real, is really mocking you for seeking to prove its reality while of your own Reality you are ignorant.

You want somehow or other to maintain that the world is real. What is the standard of Reality? That alone is Real which exists by itself, which reveals itself by itself, and which is eternal and unchanging.

Does the world exist by itself? Was it ever seen without the aid of the mind? In sleep there is neither mind nor world. When awake there is the mind and there is the world. What does this invariable concomitance mean? You are familiar with the principles of inductive logic, which are considered the very basis of scientific investigation. Why do you not decide this question of the reality of the world in the light of those accepted principles of logic?

Of yourself you can say "I exist." That is, yours is not

mere existence; it is Existence of which you are conscious. Really, it is Existence identical with Consciousness.

D. The world may not be conscious of itself, yet it exists.

M. Consciousness is always Self-consciousness. If you are conscious of anything, you are essentially conscious of yourself. Unself-conscious existence is a contradiction in terms. It is no existence at all. It is merely attributed existence, whereas true Existence, the *sat,* is not an attribute, it is the Substance itself. It is the *vastu.* Reality is therefore known as *sat-chit,* Being-Consciousness, and never merely the one to the exclusion of the other. The world neither exists by itself, nor is it conscious of its existence. How can you say that such a world is real?

And what is the nature of the world? It is perpetual change, a continuous, interminable flux. A dependent, unself-conscious, ever-changing world cannot be real.

D. Not only does Western empirical science consider the world real, but the Vedas give elaborate cosmological descriptions of the world and its origin. Why should they do so if the world is unreal?

M. The essential purpose of the Vedas is to teach you the nature of the imperishable *Ātman,* and to declare with authority, "Thou art That."

D. I accept. But why should they give cosmological descriptions spun out at great length, unless they consider the world real?

M. Adopt in practice what you accept in theory, and leave the rest. The *śastras* have to guide every type of seeker after Truth, and all are not of the same mental makeup. What you cannot accept treat as *artha-vāda* or auxiliary argument.

The Heart Is the Self

D. Śrī Bhagavan speaks of the Heart as the seat of Consciousness and as identical with the Self. What does the Heart exactly signify?

M. The question about the Heart arises because you are interested in seeking the source of consciousness. To all deep-thinking minds, the inquiry about the "I" and its nature has an irresistible fascination.

Call it by any name, God, Self, the Heart, or the Seat of Consciousness, it is all the same. The point to be grasped is this, that Heart means the very core of one's being, the center, without which there is nothing whatever.

D. But Śrī Bhagavan has specified a particular place for the Heart within the physical body, that it is in the chest, two digits to the right from the median.

M. Yes, that is the center of spiritual experience according to the testimony of Sages. This spiritual Heart-center is quite different from the blood-propelling, muscular organ known by the same name. The spiritual Heart center is not an organ of the body. All that you can say of the Heart is that it is the very core of your being: that with which you are really identical (as the word in Sanskrit literally signifies),[8] whether you are awake, asleep, or dreaming, whether you are engaged in work or immersed in *samādhi.*

D. In that case, how can it be localized in any part of the body? Fixing a place for the Heart would imply setting physiological limitations to That which is beyond space and time.

M. That is right. But the person who puts the question about the position of the Heart, considers himself as existing with or in the body. While putting the question now, would you say that your body alone is here but that you are speaking from somewhere else? No, you accept your bodily existence. It is from this point of view that any reference to a physical body comes to be made.

Truly speaking, pure Consciousness is indivisible; it is without parts. It has no form and shape, no "within" and "without." There is no "right" or "left" for it. Pure Consciousness, which is the Heart, includes all, and nothing is outside or apart from it. That is the ultimate Truth.

From this absolute standpoint, the Heart, Self, or Consciousness can have no particular place assigned to it in the physical body. What is the reason? The body is itself a mere projection of the mind, and the mind is but a poor reflection of the radiant Heart. How can That, in which everything is contained, be itself confined as a tiny part within the physical body which is but an infinitesimal, phenomenal manifestation of the one Reality?

But people do not understand this. They cannot help thinking in terms of the physical body and the world. For instance, you say, "I have come to this *aśrama* all the way from my country beyond the Himalayas." But that is not the truth. Where is a "coming" or "going" or any movement whatever, for the one, all-pervading Spirit which you really are? *You* are where you have always been. It is your body that moved or was conveyed from place to place till *it* reached this *aśrama.*

This is the simple truth, but to a person who considers himself a subject living in an objective world, it appears as something altogether visionary!

It is by coming down to the level of ordinary understanding that a place is assigned to the Heart in the physical body.

D. How then shall I understand Śrī Bhagavan's statement that the *experience* of the Heart center is at the particular place in the chest?

M. Once you accept that from the true and absolute standpoint, the Heart as pure Consciousness is beyond space and time, it will be easy for you to understand the rest in its correct perspective.

D. It is only on that basis that I have put the question about the position of the Heart. I am asking about Śrī Bhagavan's experience.

M. Pure Consciousness wholly unrelated to the physical body and transcending the mind is a matter of direct experience. Sages know their bodiless, eternal Existence just as the layman knows his bodily existence. But the experience of Consciousness can be with bodily awareness as well as without it. In the bodiless experience of pure Consciousness the Sage is beyond time and space, and no question about the position of the Heart can then at all arise.

Since, however, the physical body cannot subsist (with life) apart from Consciousness, bodily awareness has to be sustained by pure Consciousness. The former, by its nature, is limited to and can never be coextensive with the latter, which is infinite and eternal. Body consciousness is merely a monadlike, miniature reflection of the pure Consciousness with which the Sage has realized his identity. For him, therefore, body consciousness is only a reflected ray, as it were, of the self-effulgent, infinite Consciousness which is himself. It is in this sense alone that the Sage is aware of his bodily existence.

Since, during the bodiless experience of the Heart as pure Consciousness, the Sage is not at all aware of the body, that absolute experience is localized by him within the limits of the physical body by a sort of feeling-recollection made while he is with bodily awareness.

D. For men like me, who have neither the direct experience of the Heart nor the consequent recollection, the matter seems to be somewhat difficult to grasp. About the position of the Heart itself, perhaps, we must depend on some sort of guesswork.

M. If the determination of the position of the Heart is to depend on guesswork even in the case of the layman, the question is surely not worth much consideration. No, it is not on guesswork that you have to depend, it is on an unerring intuition.

D. For whom is the intuition?

M. For one and all.

D. Does Śrī Bhagavan credit me with an intuitive knowledge of the Heart?

M. No, not of the Heart, but of the position of the Heart in relation to your identity.

D. Śrī Bhagavan says that I intuitively know the position of the Heart in the physical body?

M. Why not?

D. (Pointing to himself) It is to *me* personally that Śrī Bhagavan is referring?

M. Yes. That is the intuition! How did you refer to yourself by gesture just now? Did you not put your finger on the right side of the chest? That is exactly the place of the Heart center.

D. So, then, in the absence of direct knowledge of the Heart center, I have to depend on this intuition?

M. What is wrong with it? When a schoolboy says, "It is I who did the sum correctly," or when he asks you, "Shall I run and get the book for you?," would he point to the head that did the sum correctly, or to the legs that will carry him swiftly to get you the book? No, in both cases, his finger is pointed quite naturally toward the right side of the chest, thus giving innocent expression to the profound truth that the Source of "I"-ness in him is there. It is an *unerring* intuition that makes him refer to himself, to the Heart which is the Self, in that way. The act is quite *involuntary* and *universal,* that is to say, it is the same in the case of every individual.

What stronger proof than this do you require about the position of the Heart center in the physical body?

D. But I have heard it said by a saint that his spiritual experience is felt at the place between the eyebrows.

M. As I said previously, that is the ultimate and perfect Realization which transcends subject-object relation. When that is achieved, it does not matter where the spiritual experience is felt.

D. But the question is which is the correct view of the two, namely, (1) that the center of spiritual experience is the place between the eyebrows, (2) that it is the Heart.

M. For purposes of practice you may concentrate between the eyebrows. It would then be *bhāvanā* or imaginative contemplation of the mind; whereas the supreme state of *anubhava* or Realization, with which you become wholly identified and in which your individuality is completely dissolved, transcends the mind. Then there can be no objectified center to be experienced by you as a subject distinct and separate from it.

D. I would like to put my question in slightly different words. Can the place between the eyebrows be said to be the seat of the Self?

M. You accept that the Self is the ultimate source of consciousness and that it subsists equally during all the three states of the mind. But see what happens when a person in meditation is overcome by sleep. As the first symptom of sleep his head begins to nod, which however could not happen if the Self were situated between the eyebrows or at any other place in the head.

If during sleep the experience of the Self is not felt between the eyebrows, that center cannot be called its seat without implying that the Self often forsakes its own place, which is absurd.

The fact is the *sādhaka* may have his experience at any center or *chakra* on which he concentrates his mind. But for that reason that particular place of *his* experience does not become *ipso facto* the seat of the Self.

There is an interesting story about Kamal, the son of Saint Kabir, which serves as an illustration to show that the head (and *a fortiori* the place between the eyebrows) cannot be considered the seat of the Self.

Kabir was intensely devoted to Śrī Rama, and he never failed to feed those who sang the praise of the Lord of his devotion. On one occasion, however, it so happened that he had not the wherewithal to provide food for such a gathering of devotees. For him, however, there could be no alternative except that he must somehow make every necessary arrangement before the next morning. So he and his son set out at night to secure the required provisions.

The story goes that after the father and son had removed the provisions from a merchant's house through a hole they made in the wall, the son went in again just to wake up the household and tell them, as a matter of principle, that their house had been burgled. When, having roused the household, the boy tried to make good his escape through the hole and join his father on the other side, his body stuck up in the aperture. To avoid being identified by the pursuing household (because, if detected, there would be no feeding at all of the devotees the next day), he called out to his father and told him to sever his head and take it away with him. That done, Kabir made good his escape with the stolen provisions and the son's head, which on reaching home, was hidden away from possible detection. The next day Kabir gave a feast to the *bhaktas,* quite unmindful of what had happened the previous night. "If it is Rama's will," said Kabir to himself, "that my son should die, may it prevail!" In the evening Kabir with the party set out as usual in procession into the town with *bhajana,* etc.

Meanwhile, the burgled householder made report to the king, producing the truncated body of Kamal, which gave them no clue. In order to secure its identification, the king had the body tied up prominently on the highway so that whoever claimed it or took it away (for no dead body is forsaken without the last rites being given to it by the kith and kin) might be interrogated or arrested by the police, who were posted secretly for the purpose.

Kabir and his party with the *bhajana* in full swing came by the highway, when, to the astonishment of all, Kamal's truncated body (which was considered dead as a doornail) began to clap its hands, marking time to the tune sung by the *bhajana* party.

This story disproves the suggestion that the head or the place between the eyebrows is the seat of the Self. It may also be noted that when in the battlefield the head of a soldier in action is severed from the body by a sudden and powerful stroke of the sword, the body continues to run or move its limbs as in a mock fight, just for a while, before it finally falls down dead.

D. But Kamal's body was dead hours before.

M. What you call death is really no extraordinary experience for Kamal. Here is the story of what had happened when he was younger still.

As a boy Kamal had a friend of equal age with whom he used to play games of marbles, etc. A general rule they observed between themselves was that if one of them owed the other a game or two, the same should be redeemed the next day. One evening they parted with a game to the credit of Kamal. Next day, in order to claim "the return of the game," Kamal went to the boy's house, where he saw the boy laid on the verandah, while his relatives were weeping beside him.

"What is the matter?" Kamal asked them. "He played with me last evening and also owes me a game." The relatives wept all the more, saying that the boy was dead. "No," said Kamal, "he is not dead but merely pretends to be so, just to evade redeeming the game he owes me." The relatives protested, asking Kamal to see for himself that the boy was really dead, that the body was cold and stiff. "But all this is a mere pretension of the boy, I know; so what if the body is stiff and cold? I too can become like that." So saying, Kamal laid himself down and in the twinkling of an eye was dead.

The poor relatives, who were weeping till then for the death of their own boy, were distressed and dismayed, and now began to weep for Kamal's death also. But up rose Kamal, declaring, "Do you see it now? I was as you would say dead, but I am up again, alive and kicking. This is how he wants to deceive me, but he cannot elude me like this with his pretensions."

In the end, the story goes, Kamal's inherent saintliness gave life to the dead boy, and Kamal got back the game that was due to him. The moral is that the death of the body is not the extinction of the Self. Its relation to the body is not limited by birth and death, and its place in the physical body is not circumscribed by one's experience felt at a particular place, as for instance between the eyebrows, due to the practice of *dhyāna* made on that center. The supreme state of Self-awareness is never absent; it transcends the three states of the mind as well as life and death.

D. Since Śrī Bhagavan says that the Self may function at any of the centers or *chakras* while its seat is in the Heart, is it not possible that by the practice of intense concentration or *dhyāna* between the eyebrows this center may itself become the seat of the Self?

M. As long as it is merely the stage of practice of concentration by fixing a place of controlling your attention, any consideration about the seat of the Self would merely be a theorization. You consider yourself as the subject, the seer, and the place whereon you fix your attention becomes the object seen. This is merely *bhāvanā*. When, on the contrary, you see the Seer himself, you merge in the Self, you become one with it; that is the Heart.

D. Then, is the practice of concentration between the eyebrows advisable?

M. The final result of the practice of any kind of *dhyāna* is that the object, on which the *sādhaka* fixes his mind, ceases to exist as distinct and separate from the subject. They (the subject and object) become the one Self, and that is the Heart.

The practice of concentration on the center between the eyebrows is one of the methods of *sādhana*, and thereby thoughts are effectively controlled for the time being. The reason is this: All thought is an extroverted activity of the mind; and thought, in the first instance, follows "sight"—physical or mental.

It should, however, be noted that this *sādhana* of fixing one's attention between the eyebrows must be accompanied by *japa*. Because next in importance to the *physical eye* is the *physical ear,* either for controlling or distracting the mind. Next in importance of the *eye of the mind* (that is, mental visualization of the object) is the *ear of the mind* (that is, mental articulation of speech), either to control and thereby strengthen the mind, or to distract and thereby dissipate it.

Therefore, while fixing the mind's eye on a center, as for instance between the eyebrows, you should also practice the mental articulation of a *nāma* (Name) or *mantra* (sacred syllable or syllables). Otherwise you will soon lose your hold on the object of concentration.

Sādhana as described above leads to identification of the Name, Word, or Self—whatever you may call it—with the center selected for purposes of *dhyāna*. Pure Consciousness, the Self, or the Heart is the final Realization.

D. Why does not Śrī Bhagavan direct us to practice concentration on some particular center of *chakra?*

M. Yoga Śastras say that the *sahasrāra* or the brain is the seat of the Self. Puruṣa Sūkta declares that the Heart is its seat. To enable the *sādhaka* to steer clear of possible doubt, I tell him to take up the "thread" or the clue of "I"ness or "I-am"-ness and follow it up to its source; because, firstly, it is impossible for anybody to entertain any doubt about this "I"-notion; secondly, whatever the *sādhana* adopted, the final goal is the realization of the Source of "I-am"-ness, which is the primary datum of your experience.

If you, therefore practice *Ātma-vichāra*, you will reach the Heart, which is the Self.

Aham and Aham-vṛtti

D. How can any inquiry initiated by the ego reveal its own unreality?

M. The ego's phenomenal existence is transcended when you dive into the Source wherefrom arises the *aham-vṛtti.*

D. But is not the *aham-vṛtti* only one of the three forms in which the ego manifests itself? Yoga Vasishtha and other ancient texts describe the ego as having a threefold form.

M. It is so. The ego is described as having three bodies—the gross, the subtle, and the causal—but that is only for the purposes of analytical exposition. If the method of inquiry were to depend on the ego's form, you may take it that any inquiry would become altogether impossible, because the forms the ego may assume are legion. Therefore, for purposes of *jñāna-vichāra,* you have to proceed on the basis that the ego has but one form, namely that of *aham-vṛtti.*

D. But it may prove inadequate for realizing *jñāna.*

M. Self-inquiry by following the clue of *aham-vṛtti* is just like the dog tracing its master by his scent. The master may be at some distant, unknown place, but that does not at all stand in the way of the dog's tracing him. The master's scent is an infallible clue for the animal, and nothing else, such as the clothes he wears or his build and stature, counts. To that scent the dog holds on undistractedly while searching for him, and finally it succeeds in tracing him.

D. The question still remains why the quest for the source of *aham-vṛtti,* as distinguished from other *vṛttis,* should be considered the direct means to Self-realization.

M. The word *aham* is itself very suggestive. The two letters of the word, namely A and HA, are the first and the last letters of the Sanskrit alphabet. The suggestion intended to be conveyed by the word is that it comprises all. How? Because *aham* signifies existence itself.

Although the concept of "I"-ness or "I-am"-ness is by usage known as *aham-vṛtti,* it is not really a *vṛtti* like the other *vṛttis* of the mind. Because unlike the other *vṛttis,* which have no essential interrelation, the *aham-vṛtti* is equally and essentially related to each and every *vṛtti* of the mind. Without the *aham-vṛtti* there can be no other *vṛitti,* but the *aham-vṛtti* can subsist by itself without depending on any other *vṛtti* of the mind. The *aham-vṛtti* is therefore fundamentally different from other *vṛttis.*

So, then, the search for the source of the *aham-vṛtti* is the search not merely for the basis of one of the forms of the ego but for the very source itself from which arises the "I-am"-ness. In other words, the quest for and the realization of the Source of the ego in the form of *aham-vṛtti* necessarily implies the transcendence of the ego in everyone of its possible forms.

D. Conceding that the *aham-vṛtti* essentially comprises all the forms of the ego, why should that *vṛtti* alone be chosen as the means for Self-inquiry?

M. Because it is the one irreducible datum of your experience; because seeking its source is the only practicable course you can adopt to realize the Self. The ego is said to have a causal body, but how can you make it the subject of your investigation? When the ego adopts that form, you are immersed in the darkness of sleep.

D. But is not the ego in its subtle and causal forms too intangible to be tackled through the inquiry into the source of *aham-vṛtti* conducted while the mind is awake?

M. No. The inquiry into the source of *aham-vṛtti* touches the very existence of the ego. Therefore the subtlety of the ego's form is not a material consideration.

D. While the one aim is to realize the unconditioned, pure Being of the Self, which is in no way dependent on the ego, how can inquiry pertaining to the ego in the form of *aham-vṛtti* be of any use?

M. From the functional point of view of the form, activity, or whatever else you may call it (it is immaterial, since it is evanescent), the ego has one and only one characteristic. The ego functions as the knot between the Self, which is pure Consciousness, and the physical body, which is inert and insentient. The ego is therefore called the *chit-jada granthi.* In your investigation into the Source of *aham-vṛtti,* you take the essential *chit* aspect of the ego: and for this reason the inquiry must lead to the realization of the pure Consciousness of the Self.

D. What is the relation between the pure Consciousness realized by the *jñāni* and the "I-am"-ness which is accepted as the primary datum of experience?

M. The undifferentiated Consciousness of pure Being is the Heart of *hṛdayam* which you really are, as signified by the word itself (*hṛt* + *ayam* = Heart am I). From the Heart arises the "I-am"-ness as the primary datum of one's experience. By itself it is *śuddha-sattva* in character. It is in this *śuddha-sattva svarupa* (that is, uncontaminated by *rajas* and *tamas*), that the "I" appears to subsist in the *jñāni*. . . .

D. In the *jñāni* the ego subsists in the sattvic form and therefore it appears as something real. Am I right?

M. No. The existence of the ego in any form, either in the *jñāni* or *ajñāni* is itself an appearance. But to the *ajñāni* who is deluded into thinking that the waking state and the world are real, the ego also appears to be real. Since he sees the *jñāni* act like other individuals, he feels constrained to posit some notion of individuality with reference to the *jñāni* also.

D. How then does the *aham-vṛtti* function in the *jñāni*?

M. It does not function in him at all. The *jñāni's lakṣya* is the Heart itself, because he is one and identical with that undifferentiated, pure Consciousness referred to by the Upanishads as the *prajñāna. Prajñāna* is verily *Brahman,* the Absolute, and there is no *Brahman* other than *prajñāna.*

D. How then does ignorance of this one and only Reality unhappily arise in the case of the *ajñāni?*

M. The *ajñāni* sees only the mind, which is the mere reflection of the Light of pure Consciousness arising from the Heart. Of the Heart itself he is ignorant. Why? Because his mind is extroverted and has never sought its source.

D. What prevents the infinite, undifferentiated Light of Consciousness arising from the Heart from revealing itself to the *ajñāni?*

M. Just as water in the pot reflects the enormous sun within the narrow limits of the pot, even so the *vāsanās* or latent tendencies of the mind of the individual, acting as the reflecting medium, catch the all-pervading, infinite Light of Consciousness arising from the Heart and present in the form of a reflection the phenomenon called the mind. Seeing only this reflection, the *ajñāni* is deluded into the belief that he is a finite being, the *jīva.*

If the mind becomes introverted through inquiry into the source of *aham-vṛtti,* the *vāsanās* become extinct, and in the absence of the reflecting medium the phenomenon of reflection, namely the mind, also disappears being absorbed into the Light of the one Reality, the Heart.

This is the sum and substance of all that an aspirant need know. What is imperatively required of him is an earnest and one-pointed inquiry into the source of *aham-vṛtti.*

D. But any endeavor he may make is limited to the mind in the waking state. How can such inquiry conducted in only one of the three states of the mind destroy the mind itself?

M. Inquiry into the source of *aham-vṛtti* is no doubt initiated by the *sādhaka* in the waking state of the mind. It cannot be said that in him the mind has been destroyed. But the process of self-inquiry itself will reveal that the alternation or transmutation of the three states of the mind as well as the three states themselves belongs to the world of phenomena, which cannot affect his intense, inward inquiry.

Self-inquiry is really possible only through intense introversion of the mind. What is finally realized as a result of such inquiry into the source of *aham-vṛtti* is verily the Heart as the undifferentiated Light of pure Consciousness, into which the reflected light of the mind is completely absorbed.

D. For the *jñāni,* then, there is no distinction between the three states of mind?

M. How can there be, when the mind itself is dissolved and lost in the Light of Consciousness?

For the *jñāni* all the three states are equally unreal. But the *ajñāni* is unable to comprehend this, because for him the standard of reality is the waking state, whereas for the *jñāni* the standard of Reality is Reality itself. This Reality of pure Consciousness is eternal by its nature and therefore subsists equally during what you call waking, dreaming, and sleep. To him who is one with that Reality there is neither the mind nor its three states and, therefore, neither introversion nor extroversion.

His is the ever-waking state, because he is awake to the eternal Self; his is the ever dreaming state, because to him the world is no better than a repeatedly presented phenomenon of dream; his is the ever-sleeping state, because he is at all times without the "body-am-I" consciousness.

D. Should I then consider Śrī Bhagavan as talking to me in a waking-dreaming-sleeping state?

M. Because your conscious experience is now limited to the duration of the extroversion of the mind, you call the present moment the waking state, whereas all the while your mind has been asleep to the Self, and therefore you are now really fast asleep.

D. To me sleep is a mere blankness.

M. That is so, because your waking state is a mere effervescence of the restless mind.

D. What I mean by blankness is that I am hardly aware of anything in my sleep; it is for me the same as non-existence.

M. But you did exist during sleep.

D. If I did, I was not aware of it.

M. You do not mean to say in all seriousness you ceased to exist during your sleep! (Laughing) If you went to sleep as Mr. X, did you get up from it as Mr. Y?

D. I know my identity, perhaps, by an act of memory.

M. Granting that, how is it possible unless there is a continuity of awareness?

D. But I was unaware of that awareness.

M. No. Who says you are unaware in sleep? It is your mind. But there was no mind in your sleep? Of what value is the testimony of the mind about your existence or experience during sleep? Seeking the testimony of the mind to disprove your existence or awareness during sleep is just like calling your son's evidence to disprove your birth!

Do you remember, I told you once previously that existence and awareness are not two different things but one and the same? Well, if for any reason you feel constrained to admit the fact that you existed in sleep be sure you were also aware of that existence.

What you were really unaware of in sleep is your bodily existence. You are confounding this bodily awareness with the true awareness of the Self, which is eternal.

Prajñāna, which is the source of "I-am"-ness, ever subsists unaffected by the three transitory states of the mind, thus enabling you to retain your identity unimpaired.

Prajñāna is also beyond the three states, because it can subsist without them and in spite of them.

It is that Reality that you should seek during your so-called waking state by tracing the *aham-vṛtti* to its source. Intense practice in this inquiry will reveal that the mind and its three states are unreal and that you are the eternal, infinite Consciousness of pure Being, the Self, or the Heart.

Notes

1. These are not the same as the *chakras.*

2. The acts of sleeping children, like eating and drinking, are acts only in the eyes of others and not in their own. They therefore do not really do those acts in spite of their appearing to do them.

3. The idea that one is one's body is what is called *hṛdayagranthi* (knot of the heart). Of the various knots, this knot, which binds together what is conscious with what is insentient, is what causes bondage.

4. The seven *jñāna bhūmikas* are:

śubhecchā (the desire for enlightenment)
vichāraṇa (inquiry)
tanumānasa (tenuous mind)
sattvāpatti (self-realization)
asaṃsakti (nonattachment)
padārthābhāvana (nonperception of objects)
turyaga (transcendence)

Those who have attained the last four *bhūmikas* are called *brahmavit, brahmavidvara, brahmavidvariya,* and *brahmavid variṣṭha* respectively.

5. These terms literally mean "the all," "brilliance," and "wisdom," respectively. Śrī Ramana here uses them in association with *jāgrat* (sleeping), *svapna* (dreaming), and *suṣupti* (deep sleep). *—Publisher's note*

6. The word *contemplation* is often used loosely as referring to a forced mental process, whereas *samādhi* lies beyond effort. However, in the language of Christian mysticism, *contemplation* is the synonym invariably used for *samādhi,* and it is in this sense that the word is used here.

7. The distinction between sleep, *kevala nirvikalpa sa-*

mādhi, and *sahaja nirvikalpa samādhi* can be clearly put in tabular form as given by Śrī Bhagavan:

Sleep	*Kevala Nirvikalpa Samādhi*	*Sahaja Nirvikalpa Samādhi*
1. Mind alive	1. Mind alive	1. Mind dead
2. Sunk in oblivion	2. Sunk in Light	2. Resolved into the Self
	3. Like a bucket tied to a rope and left lying in the water in a well	3. Like a river discharged into the ocean and its identity lost
	4. To be drawn out by the other end of the rope	4. A river cannot be redirected from the ocean

The mind of the Sage who has realized the Self is wholly destroyed. It is dead. But to the onlooker, he may seem to possess a mind just like the layman. Hence the "I" in the Sage has merely an apparent objective reality; in fact, however, it has neither subjective existence nor objective reality.

8. See page 103.

Glossary

ābhāsa reflection of consciousness
abhyāsa practice
Advaita the philosophical teaching of nonduality
aham "I"
ahaṃkāra "the doer"; ego
aham-vṛtti "I"-thought
aikya mukti liberation
ajñāna ignorance
ajñāni one who has not realized the Self
ānandam bliss
antar-mukha "inwardness"; retaining the mind in the Heart
anubhava experience; realization
anuṣṭhāna practice; attainment of knowledge
arthavāda auxiliary argument
ārudha attainment
asan (Skt., *asana*) posture (as in the classic positions of Hatha Yoga)
āśrama one of the four stations of life of a spiritual seeker; also, the dwelling of a sage and his disciples
ātma-jñāni one who knows the Self
Ātman the Self
ātma niṣṭha established in the Self
Atma prajñā innate self-consciousness
ātma śakti potency of the Self
ātma-siddhi Self-realization
ātma-vichāra Self-inquiry
ātma-vidya knowledge of the Self
ātma vyavahāra communion with the Self

bahir-mukha "externalization"; letting the mind go out of the Heart
bhajana worship
bhakta devotee
bhakti devotion
bhāvanā feeling of deep devotion; the contemplation of a personified deity with great emotion
bhūmikā stage
brahmachāri, brahmachārin student (one of the four stations of life)
brahmacharya state of religious students
Brahma-jñāna realization of one's absolute being
Brahman the Universal Self; the Absolute

chakras subtle centers of energy in the body
chidābhāsa reflected consciousness
chidānanda bliss of the Self
chit intelligence; consciousness
chit-jada granthi the "knot between pure consciousness and the insentient body"; the ego

dehātma-buddhi "I am the body" idea
dhātus humors; constituent elements of the body
dhyāna repetition of a mantra or name of God with devotion; meditation through deliberate mental effort
dhyāna siddhi successful meditation
Dvaita the philosophical teaching of dualism

ekānta vāsa "dwelling in solitude"; free from mental concepts

granthi nāśam destruction of the knot (of ignorance)
gṛhastha householder (one of the four stations of life)
Guru spiritual preceptor
Guru-kṛpa Guru's grace

hṛdayagranthi "knot of the heart"; the idea that one is one's body
hṛdayam the Heart

irai-pani-nittal "living in the service of God"
Īśvara God; the Lord
Īśvara-svarūpa the true form of God

jada insentient
jagat the world
jāgrat the waking state
jāgrat-suṣupti absolute quiescence; "waking sleep"; the state of being aware but not concerned
japa mental or verbal utterance of the names of God or *mantras*
jīva the individual soul
jīvanmukta realized soul
jñāna knowledge
jñāna-bhūmikās stages of knowledge
jñāna-dṛṣti wisdom-insight
jñāna grantha Vedantic works
jñāna-vichāra inquiry regarding knowledge
jñāni sage; a knower of *Brahman*

karma the collective results of one's actions; the chain of cause and effect
karma-yogi one who follows the yoga of selfless action
kartṛtva "the doer"
kevala nirvikalpa the state of remaining without concepts

lakṣya attention; aim, target

manonāśa destruction of the mind
manonigraha rendering the mind quiescent
mantra sacred syllable(s) repeated in meditation
māyā illusion
māyāśakti the power of *māyā*

mokṣa liberation
mouna (Skt., *mauna*) silence
mukti liberation

nāda sound
nāḍīs psychic nerves
nāma name
nāma-japa repetition of the name of God
namaskār (Skt., *namaskāra*) homage
nirguṇopāsana contemplation of the attributeless *Brahman*
nirvāṇa final liberation
nirvikalpa samādhi an advanced state of meditation in which there is no awareness of the world
nityam eternal
nivṛtti cessation of activity

om a mystic syllable, used as a *mantra*

para God
para-bhakti supreme devotion
paripūrṇam the perfect state
prajñā wisdom
prajñāna full consciousness
prakṛti the unmanifest (nature)
prāṇa one of the five vital airs or breaths
praṇayāma breath control
prārabdha the result of one's past actions, encountered in the present life
prasād (Skt., *prasāda*) divine blessing
pūrṇam plenum; fullness
puruṣa the Self
pūrva saṃskāras latent tendencies

ṛṣi seer; sage
rajas activity

sadguru true teacher
sādhaka spiritual aspirant
sādhana spiritual practice
sadśiṣya true disciple
sahaja jñāni sage in the state of *sahaja nirvikalpa samādhi*
sahaja nirvikalpa samādhi natural state of absorption in the Self with no concepts
sahasrāra "the thousand-petaled lotus"; one of the *chakras*
samādhi advanced state of meditation; absorption in the Self
saṃkalpas fancies
saṃsāra the bondage of life, death, and rebirth
saṃskāras past tendencies; impressions created by previous actions and thoughts
sannyāsa asceticism; renunciation
sannyasāśrama the last of the four stations of life
sannyāsin ascetic; renunciate
Sarveśvara the supreme Lord
śastras scriptures
sat existence; being
sat-chit being-consciousness
sat-chit-ānanda existence-consciousness-bliss
sattvic (from Skt. *sattva*) pure
sāyujya union; identity
siddhi accomplishment; supernatural power
śrutis sacred texts
stuti singing the praises of the Lord with devotion
śuddha-sattva svarūpa utter purity
śūnyavādin nihilist
suṣupti deep sleep
svapna the dreaming state

tadākāranilai "abiding in the form of That"; abiding in the Self
taijasa brilliance
tamas inertia

tattvas categories, principles
turīya "the fourth state" (following those of waking, dreaming, and deep sleep)
turīyātita "beyond the fourth (state)"; the Self

upadeśa instruction
upāsana contemplation

vairāgya dispassion; nonattachment
variṣṭha "the most excellent"
vāsanās impressions; latent tendencies
vāsanā-kṣaya destruction of mental tendencies
vastu substance
vichāra inquiry
vichāra mārga path of inquiry
vijñāna knowledge
vikalpas doubts
Viśiṣtādvaita qualified nondualism
viśva the all
vīveka wisdom
vṛtti mental concept

yoga spiritual path or practice; way to union with *Brahman*
yoga-māyā magical power
yoga-mārgas yogic paths
yogi follower of a path of *yoga*

Shambhala Classics

Appreciate Your Life: The Essence of Zen Practice, by Taizan Maezumi Roshi.

The Art of Peace, by Morihei Ueshiba. Edited by John Stevens.

The Art of War, by Sun Tzu. Translated by the Denma Translation Group.

The Art of Worldly Wisdom, by Baltasar Gracián. Translated by Joseph Jacobs.

Awakening to the Tao, by Liu I-ming. Translated by Thomas Cleary.

The Book of Five Rings, by Miyamoto Musashi. Translated by Thomas Cleary.

The Book of Tea, by Kakuzo Okakura.

Breath by Breath: The Liberating Practice of Insight Meditation, by Larry Rosenberg.

Cutting through Spiritual Materialism, by Chögyam Trungpa.

The Diamond Sutra and the Sutra of Hui-neng. Translated by Wong Mou-lam and A. F. Price.

The Great Path of Awakening, by Jamgön Kongtrül. Translated by Ken McLeod.

Insight Meditation: A Psychology of Freedom, by Joseph Goldstein.

The Japanese Art of War: Understanding the Culture of Strategy, by Thomas Cleary.

Kabbalah: The Way of the Jewish Mystic, by Perle Epstein.

Lovingkindness: The Revolutionary Art of Happiness, by Sharon Salzberg.

Meditations, by J. Krishnamurti.

Monkey: A Journey to the West, by David Kherdian.

The Myth of Freedom and the Way of Meditation, by Chögyam Trungpa.

Narrow Road to the Interior and Other Writings, by Matsuo Bashō. Translated by Sam Hamill.

The Places That Scare You: A Guide to Fearlessness in Difficult Times, by Pema Chödrön.

The Rumi Collection: An Anthology of Translations of Mevlâna Jalâluddin Rumi. Edited by Kabir Helminski.

(Continued on next page)

Seeking the Heart of Wisdom: The Path of Insight Meditation, by Joseph Goldstein and Jack Kornfield.

Seven Taoist Masters: A Folk Novel of China. Translated by Eva Wong.

Siddhartha, by Hermann Hesse. Translated by Sherab Chödzin Kohn.

Spiritual Teaching of Ramana Maharshi, by Ramana Maharshi.

Start Where You Are: A Guide to Compassionate Living, by Pema Chödrön.

T'ai Chi Classics. Translated with commentary by Waysun Liao.

Tao Teh Ching, by Lao Tzu. Translated by John C. H. Wu.

The Taoist I Ching, by Liu I-ming. Translated by Thomas Cleary.

The Tibetan Book of the Dead: The Great Liberation through Hearing in the Bardo. Translated with commentary by Francesca Fremantle and Chögyam Trungpa.

Training the Mind and Cultivating Loving-Kindness, by Chögyam Trungpa.

The Tree of Yoga, by B. K. S. Iyengar.

The Way of the Bodhisattva, by Shantideva. Translated by the Padmakara Translation Group.

The Way of a Pilgrim and The Pilgrim Continues His Way. Translated by Olga Savin.

When Things Fall Apart: Heart Advice for Difficult Times, by Pema Chödrön.

The Wisdom of No Escape and the Path of Loving-Kindness, by Pema Chödrön.

The Wisdom of the Prophet: Sayings of Muhammad. Translated by Thomas Cleary.

The Yoga-Sūtra of Patañjali: A New Translation with Commentary. Translated by Chip Hartranft.

Zen Lessons: The Art of Leadership. Translated by Thomas Cleary.

Zen Training: Methods and Philosophy, by Katsuki Sekida.